The Reference Shelf (*Continued*)

Volume XVIII

No.
3. Representative American Speeches: 1944-1945. A. C. Baird. $1.25.
5. Anatomy of Racial Intolerance. G. B. de Huszar. $1.25.

No.
6. Palestine: Jewish Homeland? J. E. Johnsen. $1.25.

Volume XVII

No.
4. Representative American Speeches: 1943-1944. A. C. Baird. $1.25.

No.
5. Lowering the Voting Age. J. E. Johnsen. $1.25.

Volume XVI

No.
1. Representative American Speeches: 1941-1942. A. C. Baird. $1.25.
2. Plans for a Postwar World. J. E. Johnsen. $1.25.

No.
6. Representative American Speeches: 1942-1943. A. C. Baird. $1.25.
7. Reconstituting the League of Nations. J. E. Johnsen. $1.25.

Volume XV

No.
1. Representative American Speeches: 1940-1941. A. C. Baird. $1.25.
2. Universal Military Service. R. E. Summers and H. B. Summers. $1.25.
3. Federal Regulation of Labor Unions. J. V. Garland. $1.25.

No.
6. Wages and Prices. R. E. Summers. $1.25.
7. The Closed Shop. J. E. Johnsen. $1.25.
9. Permanent Price Control Policy. J. E. Johnsen. $1.25.
10. A Federal Sales Tax. E. R. Nichols. $1.25.

Volume XIV

No.
1. Representative American Speeches: 1939-1940. A. C. Baird. $1.50.
2. Interstate Trade Barriers. J. E. Johnsen. $1.25.
6. Compulsory Military Training. J. E. Johnsen. $1.25.

No.
8. International Federation of Democracies. J. E. Johnsen. $1.25.
9. Debate Index. Supplement. J. E. Johnsen. 75c.

Volume XIII

No.
4. Europe: Versailles to Warsaw. R. S. Kain. $1.25.
5. Public Housing in America. M. B. Schnapper. $1.25.
6. United States Foreign Policy (Supplement) J. E. Johnsen. 75c.

No.
9. The National Labor Relations Act. Should It Be Amended? J. E. Johnsen. $1.25.
10. Trade Unions and the Anti-Trust Laws. J. E. Johnsen. $1.25.

THE REFERENCE SHELF

Vol. 23   No. 3

UNIVERSAL CONSCRIPTION
FOR
ESSENTIAL SERVICE

Edited by
HERBERT L. MARX, Jr.
Associate Editor, Scholastic Magazines

THE H. W. WILSON COMPANY
NEW YORK   1951

Copyright 1951
By The H. W. Wilson Company
All Rights Reserved
Printed in the United States of America

PREFACE

The marshaling of human resources in time of emergency has always been a complex problem. This is especially true in a democratic society, where pre-existing controls are not usually available to direct efforts into predetermined channels. But, as has been demonstrated in both peace and war, a democratic nation can effectively meet the challenge of emergency action.

This has certainly been true of the United States. Yet, at least in regard to war, we have had a grace period each time in which to select and train our manpower. This was the case in World War I and in World War II. Even in helping to meet the Communist onslaught in Korea, our force-in-being was sufficient to stand fast until fresh reserves could be brought in after months of training.

Will this pattern hold for a future war, in which atomic weapons may bring the arena of battle to our own land? What must we do, in terms of manpower control, to prepare against such a time?

One proposal is to subject all American citizens to conscription for essential service in time of war. This obviously includes military service, civilian labor, and such intermediate duties as civil defense and emergency police work. The proposal represents nearly complete control and direction of human resources. Up to now, however, we have progressed only part of the way toward such control and direction. How much further we could or should go in time of war is the subject of wide debate.

In the organization of civilian manpower controls, there are these successive steps:

1. Operation of the free market in labor, with no restrictions on employee or employer.
2. Ceiling limits on wages and other forms of compensation (which tend to stabilize the labor force, because the inducement of higher pay in alternate jobs is largely eliminated).

3. Restrictions on employer hiring and firing, and on employee movement from one job to another.
4. "Work or fight" orders, requiring workers to find essential civilian tasks or face induction into the armed services.
5. Direction of all workers to specific civilian or military positions.

The United States has, in the past, gone as far as the fourth step, but has never seriously contemplated the final step. For military manpower, there are these parallel steps:

1. Reliance on voluntary enlistment (used during peacetime in the past).
2. Selective service (recruitment for involuntary service of men in certain age groups and with certain qualifications).
3. Universal military training (peacetime training of all young men, preparing them for possible military service later on).
4. Universal military service (actual service in the armed forces for all young men for a specific period).
5. Unlimited military conscription (required military service without regard to age or length of enlistment of as many men as are deemed necessary).

We have already arrived at the second step in this progression, and the next two steps have been called for immediately by some groups. Step five has not been, and probably will not be, seriously considered.

This volume deals with these civilian and military manpower controls in roughly the order outlined above. The first section describes current aspects of manpower resources and controls, the second takes up present military controls, the third deals with universal military training and service, while the fourth covers the pros and cons of universal conscription (both military and civilian) for essential service. Finally, the role of women in time of emergency is assessed.

Three separate articles deal with British experiences during and since World War II. This is not intended to offer Britain as a model to be imitated. But some of the lessons learned by the British serve as a guide to American thinking about national service—as to both its merits and shortcomings.

The editor wishes to express special appreciation for suggestions and assistance in the preparation of this volume to Senator Richard B. Russell, Senator Lyndon B. Johnson, Representative Carl Vinson, Ralph E. McCoy of the Institute of Labor and Industrial Relations of the University of Illinois, Lieutenant Colonel Irving W. Hart, Chief Information Officer of the Selective Service System, and to many individuals in the Library of Congress and the Department of Labor. Acknowledgment is also gratefully made to the many authors and publishers who granted permission to reprint materials.

HERBERT L. MARX, JR.

June 18, 1951

CONTENTS

PREFACE 3

MANPOWER NEEDS IN AN EMERGENCY PERIOD
Wilson, Charles E. Our Manpower Resources 11
Truman, Harry S. Policy for Manpower Mobilization 19
Department of Labor. New Manpower Agencies 24
Drucker, Peter F. Untapped Reservoirs of Productive Capacity .... Saturday Evening Post 25
Corson, John J. Making the Most of Manpower ....
.... New York Times Magazine 30

MANPOWER FOR THE ARMED FORCES
Military Manpower Legislation of 1951 34
Armstrong, Paul G. Selective Service in History ....
.... State Government 41
Hershey, Lewis B. A Long-Range Program for Selective Service 46
Frank, Stanley. How Fair Is the Draft? ....
.... Nation's Business 49
Marx, Herbert L. Jr. Should Superior College Students Be Deferred? .... Senior Scholastic 56
Fitzpatrick, Edward A. Role of the Conscientious Objector 60

UNIVERSAL MILITARY TRAINING AND SERVICE
Editor's Introduction 63
Devan, S. Arthur. An Outline of UMT's Merits 63
President's Advisory Commission on Universal Training. A Program for National Security 67
Pratt, Fletcher. Necessity—the Basic Reason for UMT ....
.... Parents' Magazine 72
Devan, S. Arthur. An Outline of UMT's Fallacies 75

National Council Against Conscription. Jeopardizing the National Welfare 80
Myers, Alonzo F. We Must Avoid Permanent Militarization .... Parents' Magazine 83
"Triumph of the Melancholy Men" .... New York Post 87
Conant, James Bryant. Universal Military Service: A Stern Program for Survival .... Look 88
Cole, Charles Woolsey. Universal Military Service: Total Conscription Will Hurt America .... Look 91
British Information Services. Universal Military Service in Britain 94

CONSCRIPTION FOR ESSENTIAL SERVICE

Editor's Introduction 98
Elliott, William Y. Overview of Compulsory National Service 99
Roosevelt, Franklin D. FDR's Proposal for National Service, I .... Current History 106
Roosevelt, Franklin D. FDR's Proposal for National Service, II .... Vital Speeches of the Day 109
Wadsworth, James W. Jr. We Must Suspend Many Rights and Privileges .... Vital Speeches of the Day 111
Stimson, Henry L. The Same Liability for All ....
.... Vital Speeches of the Day 115
Bishop, Philip William. Effective Labor Control Needed 120
Special Senate Committee Investigating the National Defense Program. Sacrifice for Sacrifices' Sake 122
Green, William. National Service a Hindrance, Not a Help .... Vital Speeches of the Day 126
Vursell, Charles W. Unjustified Centralization of Power
.... Congressional Record 130
Wertz, Leo R. "Miracles of Production" Through Voluntary Means 133
British Ministry of Labor and National Service. National Service in Wartime Britain 136
McVoy, Edgar C. Wartime Manpower Controls in Japan
.... American Sociological Review 141

THE ROLE OF WOMEN

Stratton, Dorothy C. Our Great Unused Resource—Womanpower .... New York Times Magazine 147
Fitzpatrick, Margaret M. Women in Wartime Britain 153
Marx, Herbert L. Jr. Should Women Be Drafted for Military Service? .... Senior Scholastic 157
Eliot, George Fielding. If Women Are Drafted ....
.... Woman's Home Companion 161

BIBLIOGRAPHY 168

MANPOWER NEEDS IN AN EMERGENCY PERIOD

OUR MANPOWER RESOURCES [1]

Economic and military strength depend upon the brains and hands that develop, maintain, and operate the machines of production and defense. Fortunately we have the most highly developed skills and production "know-how" of any nation. We have also the advantage of the initiative, resourcefulness, and enterprise of a free people—the products of our democratic way of life. But in numbers our manpower resources are limited. *Therefore, if we are wasteful of our resources, manpower deficiencies could become the limiting factor in production and in military strength.*

Our work force is already almost fully employed. The number of young men of fighting age who can be marshaled is limited. Some skilled trades and professions which require long training are already in short supply. Many, if not most, of those who can be brought into our labor force, although they have latent abilities, must be trained before they can become effective.

To make the best use of our manpower resources, we, as a nation, must accomplish the following:

1. *We must distribute our manpower between the military services and the civilian economy so as to achieve the best result in terms of the national interest.*

2. *We must expand the supply of manpower available for defense production, including agriculture, until requirements are met.*

3. *We must utilize our work force at their highest skills and capacities.*

[1] From *Building America's Might*, first quarterly report to the President, by Charles E. Wilson, Director of Defense Mobilization. Government Printing Office. Washington, D.C. 1951. p23-8.

4. *We must quickly train adequate numbers for defense jobs and continue the education and training of skilled and scientific personnel.*

5. *We must provide adequate housing and community facilities and services for defense workers whenever the defense production cannot be located where the workers already live.*

6. *We must maintain our basic standards of education and health, so as to develop our manpower resources over the long run.*

Many problems that arise will be local in nature and must be solved by local action. National policies for manpower mobilization were defined by the President in a directive issued to all agencies on January 17 [1951].[2]

All of the foreseeable manpower needs for defense production can be met without using compulsory measures. The desirability of a free choice of his job on the part of each worker was reaffirmed in the President's national manpower mobilization policy. The agencies participating in programs for manpower utilization will carry out this policy.

Since the beginning of the Korean conflict, the armed forces have been expanded by more than 1.4 million men. Compared to fewer than 1.5 million last June, present [April 1, 1951] strength is more than 2.9 million—two thirds of the increase needed to meet the goal of about 3.5 million. This has been accomplished through an intensified recruitment program, recall of reserves and mobilization of National Guard units, and a revival of inductions through selective service. . . .

Certain occupational skills which are critical to the maintenance of defense production and essential civilian services have been identified in order that men possessing them may be called into the armed forces only to the extent that their skills are actually needed in military service. These skills are contained in a "List of Critical Occupations" which, along with a "List of Essential Activities," was prepared by the Departments of Commerce and Labor. The lists are used by the Department of Defense in determining who should be deferred in calling

[2] See selection below, "Policy for Manpower Mobilization."—Ed.

reserves to active duty. The Selective Service System has also distributed these lists to their local boards for their information in considering requests for occupational deferment.

The Selective Service Act was amended on September 9 [1950] to authorize the special registration, classification, and induction of certain medical, dental, and allied specialists under 50 years of age. Although the registration is complete, sufficient volunteers have made unnecessary so far any involuntary inductions under the "doctor draft."

Since the present critical world situation may last for many years, we must not deplete one of our principal assets—our highly trained personnel in many specialized fields. Enough engineers, scientists, doctors, and other specialists must continue to flow out of our colleges for replacements and to meet the increasing demands of our complex modern society.

To meet this need, a sufficient number of students will have to have their service in the armed forces postponed and be allowed to continue with their college education. Financial assistance should be provided for exceptionally qualified students unable to pay their own way. Specific plans for this purpose are now under consideration by the executive agencies and the Congress.[3]

To meet our defense production goals, the portion of the labor force engaged directly or indirectly in defense production will have to be increased by 3 to 4 million workers in 1951.

Part of this requirement may be met by a shift of workers from nondefense to defense production. However, in order to meet the requirements fully, and at the same time maintain nondefense production as fully as possible we need to add a large number of persons to the present working force as a whole.

Such an increase to the working force is feasible, despite the fact that the number of employed workers is now at record heights.

By February 1951, we had 61.3 million men and women in our civilian work force. Of these 58.9 million were employed —the largest number ever at work in February. Unemployment

[3] See selection on deferment of college students in following section.—Ed.

was down to 2.4 million, compared with the 4.7 million unemployed in February 1950.

The rise in employment in defense production has thus far been moderate, largely because of the length of time it takes to translate defense plans and appropriations into actual production and jobs. The initial employment increases occurred chiefly in industries already engaged in production of munitions and related items, such as aircraft and ordnance. With the building, expansion, or reactivation of defense plants, sharp employment gains also occurred in the machinery and related metalworking industries, as well as in industrial construction. Increased procurement of civilian-type goods, such as food and clothing items, for the growing military establishment also contributed to an expanding demand for workers.

However, during this initial phase of the defense program, employment on defense orders has been very largely superimposed on the continuing high volume of goods produced for the civilian economy. *The major part of the employment impact of the defense program upon civilian industries still lies ahead.*

The major sources of the 3 to 4 million new defense workers will be:

Transfer from Nondefense Activities. Much of the need for defense workers will be met by the transfer of workers from civilian activities. Many will shift without leaving their present job stations as their establishments convert to defense production.

Reduction of Unemployment. Although the number of unemployed workers is already relatively low, we can expect a further movement of unemployed workers into jobs as defense production accelerates.

Addition of New Workers. In recent years our labor force has grown at an average rate of nearly a million annually, due mainly to the growth in the population of working age and to the increasing employment of women. This growth will be less in the years immediately ahead because of the increased requirements of military service. . . . About 38 million persons of working age and not in school are not in the labor force. Of these, 5 million [are] . . . men and 33 million women. Important reserves of manpower are available among housewives with grown children, older persons near the conventional retirement age, and the handicapped. If industry adapts its hiring practices and job standards to utilize these sources of manpower, we can add an additional million workers or more from these sources this year.

Increased Hours of Work. For each hour of overtime added to the workweek in manufacturing establishments, we would gain the production equivalent of almost 350,000 new workers. The workweek in manufacturing industries averaged about 41 hours in February 1951. Many workers are still employed less than 40 hours, although some workweeks as high as 48 hours are in effect. For example, in December a majority of workers in machine tools and copper mining industries were already on scheduled workweeks of 48 hours or more. The 41-hour average compares to a peak of $45\frac{1}{2}$ hours in World War II when many industries were on a 48-hour schedule.

There are, of course, definite limits to the extent to which production can be increased by increasing overtime. Absenteeism and declines in efficiency begin to cut in heavily after about 48 hours a week is reached.

United States Employment Service and the affiliated state employment services are already proving of invaluable assistance to employers and workers in the orderly filling of defense jobs. Preferential service is being extended to employers with defense contracts or in activities which the government is encouraging to expand.

With agricultural production goals set higher than ever before, there will be an increased demand for farm workers at a time when inductions into the armed forces and the attractions of defense jobs will reduce the supply of farm workers. The farm placement service of the public employment system has accordingly expanded and intensified its recruitment program.

The President's national manpower policy calls for full use of domestic manpower resources before foreign workers are brought in. The domestic supply of certain types of harvest labor, however, has never been entirely adequate since World War II. and arrangements are now being made for the increased numbers of foreign workers who will be required as the manpower situation tightens.

The large-scale migration of workers during World War II led to congestion and overtaxed housing, health, educational and other community facilities, and services in many localities. To avoid these consequences in the current program, the government agencies concerned are taking steps to see that the labor supply in nonshortage areas will be used as fully as possible before additional jobs are created in areas of labor shortage. The Secretary of Defense [has] . . . directed the military departments to pay particular attention to the availability of manpower, in letting defense contracts.

In addition, every private employer is urged to follow the same policy in the placement of subcontracts, in the ordering of materials, and in the securing of services. Particularly, every employer should utilize local labor supplies to the utmost before undertaking out-of-area recruitment. Where the local labor supply is inadequate, workers can be recruited from other areas in the state or from areas outside the state through the clearance system of the public employment service.

The movement of workers from jobs in less essential industries or services to defense plants should be encouraged, but "pirating" of workers by one defense plant from another should be avoided.

Movement of workers into defense industries will be impeded unless reemployment rights of transferred workers can be preserved and their seniority, pension, and insurance rights protected. Labor, management, and government groups are working to formulate solutions.

Most of the defense-production industries undergoing rapid expansion in the months ahead have historically had a higher wage structure than many other sectors of the economy. This will be an important factor in recruiting workers for these industries, although the differentials are less than they were in World War II. Experience during World War II indicates, too, that the longer average workweek in defense plants (with premium overtime pay) and greater opportunities for training and advancement were also important factors in attracting workers.

If in unusual cases, however, these incentives prove insufficient to prevent serious manpower shortages in critical defense industries, adjustments in wages can be allowed under the wage-stabilization regulations.

Many American workers are still employed in jobs which do not utilize their skills to the fullest extent. Efficient use of manpower requires the wider application of progressive personnel policies, upgrading, training, and advanced techniques in labor relations and human relations.

To secure maximum utilization of his work force, each employer, private and public, should—

1. Make the maximum use of skills of manpower already employed, including the systematic upgrading of workers to higher skill levels, the relaxation of retirement policies, and the modification of job specifications to eliminate underutilization of persons with needed skills, particularly among minority groups.

2. Keep manpower working full time and at peak productivity by providing favorable working conditions, health and safety programs, minimizing time lost due to production factors, and eliminating unnecessary work.

3. Retain the present working force by minimizing those factors which contribute to turnover.

4. Establish effective assignment, induction, and training programs for newly employed workers.

5. Use part-time workers.

To assist employers in achieving these objectives, the public employment service has expanded its program of technical service in manpower utilization.

Two types of training are required to meet defense production requirements:

1. Training for immediate production needs—introductory training on the job of new workers, refresher training for those returning to the labor market, and instruction required as a result of shifts from nondefense industries or upgrading of workers in the plant.

2. Training for longer-range needs—for the skilled trades and for scientific, technical, and professional pursuits.

In meeting the immediate production needs, the primary responsibility for training his workers rests with the employer. The Department of Labor's "skill improvement program" is available to give him such assistance as he requests for in-plant training. In addition, the federal-state vocational education system will provide instructional personnel, materials, or facilities for defense training when they are beyond the capacity of individual employers. In this way, the needed training will be tailored to the needs in each locality and each plant.

As for the longer-range training needs, acute shortages have already appeared in some crafts. The Department of Labor, in cooperation with management and labor and state agencies, is expanding and accelerating its apprenticeship program to assure a sufficient number of craftsmen, especially in critical occupations.

Experience in World War II demonstrated that housing shortages, inadequate public health measures, crowded schools and hospitals, overtaxed shopping and recreational facilities, and a lack of child-care facilities and services not only lowered workers' efficiency, but made it difficult to retain the manpower recruited for defense industries.

Despite our general policy of bringing the work to the worker, other overriding considerations have already made it necessary to expand employment in several congested areas . . . and in a few instances in areas where housing and other community facilities and services are practically nonexistent. The latter is particularly true in the case of the Atomic Energy Commission projects at Paducah, Kentucky, and on the Savannah River in South Carolina.

To meet the problem of these and similar localities, an interagency Critical Area Committee has been established under the Defense Production Administration to designate "critical defense areas" and to consider steps to minimize the impact of the defense program.

Credit controls on private housing construction are being relaxed in such areas in order to stimulate production of part of the housing needed. The disposition of the remaining 300,000 units of war housing constructed by the government during

World War II has been halted, unused units reopened where needed, and priority for occupancy given to defense workers.

In a long-term defense program, we cannot neglect the maintenance of our general standards of health and education without a loss of ultimate strength.

Sickness keeps about a million workers off the job every day. We cannot afford this waste of manpower.

In order to maintain health standards, it is estimated that by 1954 we must train 21,000 physicians, 9,000 dentists, and 50,000 nurses more than are now practicing or being trained. Our training institutions in these fields must therefore be immediately expanded. This will require private, local, state, and federal cooperation. . . .

The men and women who will be needed in the future for military service, for the factories and the farms are the children now in primary and secondary schools. In view of the long-range character of the defense program, it is important that we develop further the present American system of local, state, and federal cooperation for meeting our educational responsibilities. In this connection, the need of eliminating overcrowding of schools and of providing adequate educational equipment and staff must be weighed against the other competing claims for scarce materials and manpower during the emergency period. Prompt action is particularly necessary where schools are overburdened because of the growth of defense activities.

POLICY FOR MANPOWER MOBILIZATION [4]

There is hereby promulgated, effective [January 17, 1951, a] National Manpower Mobilization Policy which I have approved on the recommendation of the National Security Council, the Secretary of the Treasury, the Secretary of Labor and the Director of the Office of Defense Mobilization.

This policy shall be adhered to by all departments and agencies with respect to programs under their control, subject

[4] From memorandum issued by President Harry S. Truman to the heads of all executive departments and agencies, January 17, 1951. Mimeographed and released to the press. The White House. Washington, D.C. 1951.

to such amendments and supplements as may from time to time be issued by the Director of the Office of Defense Mobilization pursuant to authorities vested in him.

Aims of Manpower Mobilization

1. The primary aim of manpower mobilization is to safeguard our national security through the maximum development and use of our human resources. In particular, this involves:

   a. Providing manpower for the armed forces in sufficient numbers and with the mental, physical, and occupational qualifications necessary for national defense.

   b. Providing manpower for producing the materials and services necessary to the armed forces, to meet commitments of aid to other nations and to support the civilian economy.

   c. Constantly increasing our mobilization potential through training and educational programs to expand our supply of persons with highly developed skills essential to civilian and military activities. Providing manpower for protection of the civilian health and welfare.

2. The most efficient use of the nation's manpower will be of vital importance in any prolonged effort to keep the strength of the United States at a high level and will be of the utmost importance in the event of full mobilization. Consequently, it is important that manpower measures taken now be consistent with and contribute to the most advantageous use of our manpower should full mobilization become necessary.

3. We must rely heavily on science and technology. The most effective use must be made of our supply of individuals having the special skills required to develop and produce the necessary equipment and to use and maintain it in the armed forces. Malutilization of such individuals represents a direct and unnecessary reduction of our defense potential.

4. While recognizing the very high priority of the armed forces' requirements for certain numbers and classes of manpower, the needs of mobilization also require a vigorous civilian economy. The manpower necessary to defense production, to civil

UNIVERSAL CONSCRIPTION

defense, to agriculture, and to the production of essential civilian goods and services and to sustain our commitments of aid to other nations, must be considered as integral parts of a balanced mobilization program.

5. To assure the most effective use of our manpower to meet these needs, it is essential that we establish principles and adopt a series of policies which will lead to the most effective use of our manpower resources. Wherever statutory authorization is necessary to put these into effect, it will be sought from the Congress.

Principles of Manpower Mobilization

6. In achieving these objectives, the national manpower mobilization program will be based upon the following principles:

    a. Each individual will be expected to serve in the capacity in which he can contribute most to the total mobilization program.

    b. Employers, both private and governmental, will assure full utilization of those abilities and skills of each individual which will contribute most to the total mobilization program through such measures as minimum manning, training, and assignment of duties in accordance with needs, skills, and potentialities.

    c. The government will develop and administer manpower programs designed to enlist to the fullest possible extent the support and resourcefulness of individuals in the achievement of the mobilization program.

Basic Manpower Mobilization Policies

7. The following basic manpower mobilization policies are necessary to give effect to the principles stated above, but do not prejudice or limit extension of manpower policies as further needs of mobilization evolve:

    a. The size of the armed forces will be determined by the President. He will be provided with the Department of

Defense requirements to meet strategic plans; with full information on the prospective supplies of manpower, and on the manpower requirements for defense production, agriculture, civil defense, and other essential purposes.

b. The greatest care must be exercised to assure that the supply of persons possessing critical skills will be distributed among military and civilian activities in a manner which will contribute most to the mobilization program. When the total need for workers with critical skills for civilian and military assignments is expected to exceed the supply that can be made available, the requirements for persons with such skills will be reviewed and distribution of the supply will be measured by the relative urgency of the need for critical skills as between the armed forces and the civilian economy.

c. Policies in respect to recruitment of individuals from civilian life and call-up of members of the unorganized reserves will have as their objective the use of persons possessing irreplaceable skills where they can make their maximum contribution to the total mobilization program.

d. Policies governing occupational deferment of persons subject to induction under the Selective Service Act, will provide for (1) the occupational deferment of persons possessing critical skills if they are currently using such skills in essential activities, except to the extent the military services require persons with those skills; (2) deferment of a sufficient number of individuals in educational and training institutions to provide an adequate continuing supply of professional and highly skilled manpower.[5]

e. Recruitment, placement, distribution, training and utilization of the civilian labor force (including government employees) will be based primarily upon voluntary measures for manpower mobilization. This policy will be carried out through such measures as (1) providing appropriate employment information to guide workers to jobs in which they can make their maximum contribution; (2) developing recruit-

---

[5] See selection on deferment of college students in following section.—Ed.

ment and rehabilitation activities needed to expand the labor force; (3) training persons to meet civilian manpower requirements and providing appropriate placement services; (4) providing assistance to employers in promoting maximum utilization of the labor force including women, physically handicapped, older workers, and minority groups; (5) providing adequate housing and community services; and (6) assisting workers to arrange for their transfer to essential jobs in other areas.

f. Governmental manpower controls will be used when and to the extent needed to assure successful execution of the mobilization program. Such controls will apply to employers, to workers, or to both. They will include (1) restricting indiscriminate labor turnover through control of separations; (2) giving effect to manpower allocations by placing employment ceilings on employers with respect to the total number of workers, the number of men or the number in particular skills; (3) controlling of employer hiring; and (4) enforcing adherence to utilization standards, including full use of women, handicapped workers, and minority groups.

g. All manpower programs will be geared to the needs and problems of specific geographical areas.

h. As mutually desirable to the United States and friendly nations, workers will be brought into the United States for, or their services utilized within the borders of their own country on, work of value to the mobilization program. Full use of domestic manpower resources will be made before bringing in foreign workers.

i. Production will be scheduled, materials allocated, and procurement distributed with careful consideration of available manpower. Whenever feasible from an economic and security standpoint, production facilities, contracts, and significant subcontracts will be located at the sources of labor supply in preference to moving the labor supply.

j. The full understanding and assistance of labor organizations, employer associations, professional societies, civic and community groups and state and local governments will be sought in carrying out these functions.

k. Each department will, itself, implement the policy and be responsible for its supervision.

NEW MANPOWER AGENCIES [6]

Defense Mobilization Director Charles E. Wilson and Secretary of Labor Maurice J. Tobin issued orders [on May 1, 1951] . . . tying together labor, management and government on manpower policy and problems through national, regional and local industrial area committees.

Wilson's order established a Labor-Management Policy Committee within the Office of Defense Mobilization, co-chaired by Arthur S. Flemming of ODM and the Labor Department's Defense Manpower Administrator, Dr. Frank P. Graham.

Tobin's amended manpower order designated the thirteen regional directors of the Department's Bureau of Employment Security to be regional directors of the Defense Manpower Administration, and also as co-chairmen of the interagency (governmental) Regional Committees on Defense Mobilization. He reissued his previous order naming the regional directors as chairmen of eight-man regional labor-management committees, already in process of establishment, and providing for area committees of persons appointed by the Secretary of Labor on nomination of labor and management leaders.

The Wilson order establishing the Labor-Management Manpower Policy Committee provides that the Committee "will have referred to it all questions of policy relative to the mobilization, training and maximum utilization of manpower in the defense program, and shall make recommendations as to the action which in its judgment should be taken by the Office of Defense Mobilization." The Committee may also volunteer recommendations.

This order means that before policy decisions are made in the manpower field by the Office of Defense Mobilization, recommendations will be made both by the Labor-Management

[6] Department of Labor press release, May 1, 1951. Mimeographed. Department of Labor. Washington, D.C. 1951.

UNIVERSAL CONSCRIPTION 25

Manpower Policy Committee and by the already existing Manpower Policy Committee. The latter consists of representatives of government agencies with operating responsibilities in the manpower field.

The regional and area labor-management committees are established, according to the Tobin order, "to obtain the advice, cooperation and leadership of management and labor in the solution of manpower problems at the regional and area levels . . ." and "to advise and assist in bringing about community understanding of such manpower problems and bringing about community action necessary to their solution."

UNTAPPED RESERVOIRS OF PRODUCTIVE CAPACITY [7]

Where will the economic shoe pinch the most as we move toward industrial mobilization? . . . The commodity which may be scarcest is one for which we were comfortably fixed last time: manpower. And our one reservoir of increased production is something we paid scant attention during World War II: worker productivity and worker morale. . . .

That employee attitude is a large and almost untapped reservoir of productive capacity we know beyond doubt. For the last twenty five years there has been steady research in this field —in our major universities, in a good many companies, and in some unions. The much-publicized employee-relations plan of the Lincoln Electric Company, in Cleveland, for example, has consistently kept workers' output some 50 per cent above the average for the industry. The plan is based on a combination of profit-sharing bonuses and careful encouragement of teamwork, producing in the worker the conviction that the plant is his plant, the job his job, the product his product. The Lincoln Electric situation is, perhaps, unique. But very large though less startling increases in output have been obtained by such different companies as Sears, Roebuck in its retail stores; Johnson and

[7] From "What Will We Be Short of This Time?" by Peter F. Drucker, consulting economist and author. *Saturday Evening Post.* 223:29. September 16, 1950. Reprinted by permission. This selection is the concluding portion of an overall survey of manpower resources.—Ed.

Johnson, the surgical-dressing manufacturers; and the large West Coast pulp-and-paper company, Crown Zellerbach.

There are three equally important ways to tap this reservoir of additional output. The first one is to pick the right man, to put him where he will be most satisfied and most productive, and to train him right: selection, placement and training. Of these, placement may be the most important, and it's the one we do the least about.

The second major factor in worker skill and worker attitude is the worker's immediate boss, the foreman. To the worker, the foreman is "management." On the foreman's knowledge of the job, on his ability and training, and above all on his capacity for leadership, depend the worker's performance.

Finally there are management's policies. They alone can make the worker feel like a real partner in the work rather than a number on the payroll. The difference between a plant with an average worker morale and one with high morale is the difference between a plant in which the worker says "They" and one in which he says "We" when he talks about what goes on. This cannot be achieved by good intentions, the golden rule or pious speeches. It requires almost a new way of life on the part of management, and many of the new policies don't come easy to some managements.

Contrary to popular belief, a war does not automatically create good worker morale. While the worker feels that his war work counts and that the nation depends on it, while it is obviously more glamorous to make hinges for fighter-plane cockpits than for automobile doors, a war also brings a great many new disturbances and pressures. People are moved around—from unessential to essential job, from plant to plant—so rapidly that they never feel at home. There is constant pressure for more work, more production. The sheer process of living becomes more difficult. An overcrowded bus, for instance, may make a man tired and sour before he even starts on the job. And, further, war work is jerky. As soon as a plant has worked up to high pitch, the army is likely to change the design of whatever the men are working on, and the whole nerve-racking business of redesigning, with its spells of hectic idleness, of changing machines and production lines, of learning a new way of doing the job, begins all over again.

We cannot trust the "excitement of a war" or the "patriotism of the American worker" to ease our manpower headache. We have to go after worker skill and worker morale seriously and systematically. It is perhaps our biggest job today. What we need first are some government policies in the manpower field—something more than the assumption that things will be very much the way they were in World War II.

One thing to think through is the possibility of using the very large manpower reserves outside the United States: in Latin America, in Western Europe and in the Pacific. It may well be easier and cheaper—let alone faster—to train and use some of that manpower than it would be to try to squeeze more out of our limited human resources.

Another policy that must be soon thought through is whether we can afford to drain off all our best young men into the armed forces or whether we have to keep a large number—perhaps even more than there are today—of our young people in school and college. If we expect to have to live for another 10 years in today's kind of uncertain world, we certainly cannot afford any decrease in the number of people in training for technical, intellectual or spiritual leadership. But it is also true that the same boy who is the best material for college is the best material for military service, and badly needed for it.

We shall have to make a similar decision with regard to foremen. One of the greatest differences between our situation today and our situation ten years ago is that we now possess a very much larger and very much better trained body of supervisors. In numbers the group is at least twice as large as it was in 1939. Then, in some automobile plants, one foreman was supposed to supervise three hundred men—an obvious absurdity. Today in the same plants there is one foreman to every 18 men. The difference in training and competence between today's foreman and the foreman of 1939 is probably even greater. For industry has learned that the foreman is the key to efficiency and productivity.

But precisely because most of our foremen are new, most of them are young. In one of the large electrical companies, for instance, where two thirds of the foremen have come up since 1943, the men under 35 represent almost one half of the total foreman group. Also, today's foremen are mostly well skilled technically. They have been trained to lead men. In other words, in age, skill and experience they are exactly what the armed forces are looking for. If we allow a draft to drain off this reservoir, industrial productivity would plummet—so much so that draft exemption for all trained and experienced supervisors would seem a sensible policy to adopt. But can we afford to withhold from the armed forces their best potential technicians and junior officers?

Thirdly, we need, urgently, a systematic program of placing older people in those jobs where their experience, judgment and emotional balance would count for more than physical strength or speed. During the next 10 years the number of people over 60 will increase by a full third—to 23 million. At the same time the number of people of normal working age—18 to 60—will, at best, remain the same, if not go down slightly. In an emergency our ability to employ older people to best advantage may become crucial. In the right place, the older man or woman is actually a good deal more productive and efficient than a younger person. But it takes thought to find that spot, and effort to place the older worker in it. . . .

One decision is clear: the first things to be cut down, should things get rough, would be residential building and automobile production. But should these really be the first things? Worker attitude is largely made within the plant or the office. But we know that two outside factors have a powerful influence: how the worker and his family are housed, and how hard it is to get to and from the place of work.

Housing and transportation are the two major areas of the economy where we are conspicuously worse off than before World War II. It is only reasonable to assume that industrial mobilization will mean large movements of people; it always does. And there is the new possibility that we may have to evacuate people. We should, in other words, have a big surplus of housing rather than a sizable shortage. It may be foolish to keep on building at the present boom scale. But then we should

—if at all possible—stock-pile building materials, perhaps prefabricated walls, partitions, windows and roofs, certainly furnaces, ranges, sinks, plumbing and refrigerators. We still have a shortage of some 3 million housing units—about two years' building at top speed—we should have a 3 million surplus in reserve to be well prepared.

The transportation picture may be even worse—not so much for goods, soldiers or war material, as for workers. More than half of our automobiles are still of prewar vintage—that is, at least 10 years old. It would take another two and a half years of the present record production of 9 million cars a year to get us back into the shape we were in when we stopped car production in 1942. And if we can't keep up the production of new automobiles that long or that high, we ought to have a huge stock pile of spare parts to keep the old cars on the road for an indefinite period. Unhappily, we are worse off for replacement parts than for new cars.

If we let building and transportation go, we may be in for a real drop in production. Not only may the morale of the whole work force suffer badly; it may be physically impossible to get all the workers we have to the places where they are needed. But building and automobile production also require the most critical raw materials, and the automobile plants are our No. 1 arsenal.

Poor government policies will make it impossible to do the job. But even the very best government effort would not get the job done. The human mobilization of a defense economy is up to management just as was the technical production job of World War II. How much of the reservoir of skill, ability and initiative that lies in the American people we shall be able to use will depend upon the skill, imagination and enterprise of individual managements all through the country.

The foundations are there. We have learned a tremendous lot during the last war and since. American industry now accepts it as proved that the proper use of its human resources is as important a job, and contributes as much directly to productivity, efficiency and profits, as the use of any other resource. Most of the larger and many smaller companies have special departments to study employee relations and to work out new and better ways of building worker skill and worker morale.

Yet we still do very little in the area, however much we may talk about it. Employee relations today is in about the same position industrial research was in just after World War I. Everybody is for it, but few do anything about it. The difference in performance between the few leaders in the field and the average well-managed company is many times greater than the difference in technical and engineering competence between the very best and the very worst of our businesses. But it is precisely for this reason that we can hope to reap the very largest harvest from a little effort in building up worker skill and worker attitude. In the last war the great achievement of American management lay in the technical field: the management of things. This time our "production miracle" will have to be based on the leadership of men.

MAKING THE MOST OF MANPOWER [8]

Because present mobilization methods offer only the prospect of hit-or-miss job placement for several million persons, most manpower officials in Washington foresee [in the immediate future] . . . high turnover, constant pressure to relax efforts to stabilize wages, pirating of workers, scarcity of skilled craftsmen and lost production. With procurement of defense materials piling up at an increasing pace, more and more contractors are seeking workers wherever they can. Most contractors try to keep their peacetime operations going at capacity and will "raid" other plants for the men needed for the defense contract. In short, damaging confusion seems certain, at least in the key industrial centers.

The prospect points up the need for additional steps to insure the orderly redistribution of our manpower and for better use of the existing supply. Eventually the government may have to freeze workers in jobs, fix employment ceilings on em-

[8] From an article by John J. Corson, director of the U. S. Employment Service in World War II. New York *Times Magazine*. p 12+. May 13, 1951. Reprinted by permission.

ployers, require employers to hire through public employment offices and insist on greater use of women and handicapped persons.

But other things are needed now. . . .

To . . . make the best use of our manpower, it is essential that the following steps be taken:

(1) Both employers and government must abandon the "business as usual" view that there is an abundance of manpower. This means that employers must use available workers as effectively as possible and not "hoard" people on peacetime activities. It means that the Defense Department must give increasing recognition to the growing scarcity of designers, machine-tool and layout men and other skilled workers, and to the necessity of deferring skilled reservists. It must take into account increasingly the local labor supply before placing contracts. It also means that the Defense Production Administration must consider what effect each of its actions has on our manpower resources.

(2) We must increase the productivity of workers now employed in order to make up the estimated deficit of about half a million workers needed under present military plans. Greater productivity can be had not only . . . by better utilization and training, but as well by lengthening hours of work and by building workers' interest and zeal—that is, by helping workers to understand the urgency of the need for defense materials and the stakes involved. The manpower problem, after all, is not merely a matter of numbers; it is primarily one of greater production.

(3 We must establish order in an increasing number of metropolitan areas where unskilled labor is becoming scarce. Regional defense mobilization committees have already been prescribed. . . . They would bring together the various agencies involved in the manpower problem—regional representatives of the Defense Production Administration, the United States Employment Service, the Department of Agriculture and other governmental agencies, and procurement representatives of the armed services. The Department of Labor has provided for other local committees which would bring together representa-

tives of management and labor to consider how available manpower can be distributed in more orderly fashion. As yet both sets of committees exist only on paper.

Through such local manpower mobilization committees much was accomplished during World War II. Through their use we could be assured again of the maximum use of the unemployed, of women, older persons, and youths who have never held jobs. Employers would be stimulated to develop training programs for the induction of such workers. They would be encouraged to inventory their personnel and plan the replacement of prospective draftees, reservists and guardsmen. Even more important, the cooperating employers and labor could effectively combat labor pirating, absenteeism, high turnover and the related wastes of vital manpower which have now begun to appear.

(4) A government agency, equal in status to the Defense Production Administration or the Economic Stabilization Agency, should be established to insure orderly redistribution of manpower. The agency should be capable of expansion in order to apply whatever controls might be needed in the event of all-out war. For the present it should influence rather than control. The present "policy committee" could be a nucleus for the agency but a stronger instrument will be needed to arbitrate the squabbles that will inevitably arise over the allocation of available manpower between military and civilian needs, to prevent the placement of defense production contracts in centers where manpower becomes scarce, and especially to create the machinery and undertake the successive actions essential to the effective mobilization of industrial manpower. New workers will not be brought into jobs, employers' standards will not be adjusted, and training classes will not be formed by a "policy committee" alone.

(5) We must face up to all the implications of the indefinite mobilization on which we are launched. We may not be able to achieve our defense goals and at the same time continue to produce as many automobiles, radios, refrigerators and nylons as we now turn out. Yet if we are destined to live in a garrison state for a decade or a generation, we cannot plan our mobilization at the cost of fewer school buildings, fewer hospitals and

fewer homes. This is the peculiar and important characteristic which differentiates the mobilization of the 1950s from that of the 1940s.

This country cannot afford to plan the mobilization of its manpower on the theory that sufficed for World War II: that manpower can be drawn from any and all peacetime pursuits to win a short war. If we must face the stark prospect of indefinite mobilization, then a regard for the individual rights of the generation coming of age as well as for the civilization of the 1970s demands that we budget our manpower for all scientific, professional and cultural pursuits as well as for military strength and defense production.

Even though our manpower supplies are adequate, if wisely used, time is short and the prospect of an even greater emergency is present. Decisive, position action on manpower should be the next item on the agenda of defense.

MANPOWER FOR THE ARMED FORCES

MILITARY MANPOWER LEGISLATION OF 1951 [1]

DRAFTING OF MEN FOR SERVICE IN THE ARMED FORCES

1. Termination of authority to draft men into the armed forces. The authority to induct men into the armed forces has been extended for 4 years, to terminate on July 1, 1955. . . .

2. Period of service. The period of service for persons inducted into the armed forces will be 24 months, an increase of 3 months over the [previous] . . . period of service. . . .

3. Registration. All male citizens of the United States and every other male person now or hereafter in the United States between the ages of 18 and 26 are required to register. Classification for induction purposes will take place as soon as practicable following registration. . . .

4. Draft age. The draft age has been reduced from 19 years to 18 years and 6 months for all male citizens of the United States and all other male persons admitted to the United States for permanent residence. All other persons who remain in the United States in a status other than that of permanent residents for a period exceeding one year, except those exempt from registration, shall be liable for training and service. Persons admitted to the United States other than as permanent residents who remain in the United States for more than one year may request

---

[1] From conference report to accompany S. 1 (Report No. 535, 82d Congress, First session, House of Representatives). House of Representatives. Washington, D.C. 1951. p16-27.

This report details the changes in the Selective Service Act of 1950, which was scheduled to expire July 9, 1951. The new law, the Universal Military Training and Service Act of 1951, covers both the extension of selective service and the initial steps of a universal military training program. The UMT provisions are, however, subject to further debate by Congress before such a program goes into operation. The 1951 Act was passed by Congress with heavy bipartisan majorities in both houses and approved by the President in June 1951. The pros and cons of UMT are discussed in a later section of this volume.—Ed.

release from training and service, but such a request will debar them from citizenship.

No person shall be inducted into the armed forces below the age of 19 by any local board so long as there are available within that local board eligible males between the ages of 19 through 25. . . .

5. *Reduction of physical and mental standards.* The physical standards for induction will be those that prevailed in January of 1945; the mental standards will be established on the basis of a percentile score of 10 which corresponds to the previously used General Classification Test of 65. The new mental standards are a reduction of 3 from the [previous] . . . percentile score of 13 and correspond to a reduction of 5 points from the previous standard of 70 heretofore established by law as a minimum General Classification Test score for induction. . . .

6. *Ceiling on the armed forces.* Until July 31, 1954, the active-duty strength of the armed forces shall not exceed more than 5 million persons at any one time. . . .

7. *Total obligated service.* All persons entering the armed forces or the National Security Training Corps [see below] after the proposed legislation is enacted will be required to serve a total obligated period of service of 8 years. This requirement applies to all persons inducted, enlisted, or appointed in the armed forces, or inducted into the National Security Training Corps. The total period of obligated service includes active duty, training duty in the National Security Training Corps, and active or inactive service in the reserve components. . . .

8. *Active duty for reservists.* All reservists and retired personnel now or hereafter ordered to active duty may be required to serve 24 months. The authority of the President to order reservists and retired personnel to active duty is extended until July 1, 1953. . . .

9. *Release of reservists.* Unless sooner released under regulations prescribed by the respective Secretaries, any member of the Inactive or Volunteer Reserve who served for a period of 12 months or more between December 7, 1941, and September 2, 1945, shall, upon application, be released to inactive duty after he has completed 17 months of active duty including the time

spent on active duty since June 25, 1950. Such persons shall not thereafter be ordered to active duty, without their consent, for a period in excess of 30 days, except in time of war or national emergency hereafter declared by the Congress. However, reservists found by the military departments concerned to possess a rating or specialty which is critical may be retained for the period for which they are ordered to active duty if their release prior to the completion of such period of time would impair the efficiency of the military department concerned. This provision applies to officers and enlisted personnel. . . .

10. *Deferment of students.* High school students will be deferred until they graduate from high school or attain the age of 20. College students may be deferred until they complete their academic year but if they are deferred to complete an academic year they may not thereafter be deferred by statute to complete an academic year. No local board may be required to defer any college student based upon a government-sponsored test score or upon the student's class standing. . . .

11. *Overseas assignment.* Every person inducted into the armed forces shall be given a period of not less than 4 months of training and may not be assigned for duty in any installation located on land outside the United States, its territories, or possessions, until after this 4-month period has elapsed. In addition, no other member of the armed forces who is enlisted, appointed, inducted, or ordered to active duty shall be assigned to duty at any installation located on land outside the United States, its territories, or possessions, until he has had the equivalent of 4 months of basic training. . . .

12. *Enlistment in the regular army.* Men between the ages of 18 years and 6 months and 26 years shall be offered an opportunity to enlist in the regular army for a period of 24 months and may not have their enlistments involuntarily extended except in time of war or national emergency. . . .

13. *Extension of voluntary enlistments.* The authority to involuntarily extend enlistments in the regular and reserve components of the armed forces is extended until July 1, 1953. Thus, all enlistments which expire after July 9, 1951, may be extended by the President for 12 months, but no person shall have his

enlistment extended more than once. Existing law extends all such enlistments which expire between July 27, 1950, and July 9, 1951. . . .

14. *Aliens.* All aliens admitted for permanent residence in the United States shall be immediately liable for induction into the armed forces or the National Security Training Corps under the same conditions applicable to citizens. Aliens admitted to the United States, other than as permanent residents, who remain in the United States for one year or more shall be liable for induction unless they request release from service. In the event that such persons request release from service, they will be debarred from citizenship. . . .

15. *Conscientious objectors.* Persons who are found by local boards to be opposed to noncombatant service shall be ordered by their local boards, subject to regulations prescribed by the President, to perform civilian work contributing to the maintenance of the national health, safety, or interest for a period of 24 months. A conscientious objector's refusal to perform such work will subject him to the penalties of the Selective Service Act. . . .

16. *Deferment of certain persons whose occupation is necessary for the maintenance of the national health, safety or interest.* The President is authorized under such regulations and rules as he may prescribe to provide for the deferment from training and service or from training in the National Security Corps of any or all categories of persons whose activity in study, research, or medical, dental, veterinary, optometric, osteopathic, scientific, pharmaceutical, chiropractic, chiropodial, or other endeavors is found to be necessary to the maintenance of the national health, safety, or interest. . . .

17. *Control over the sale, consumption, possession of, or traffic in, beer, wine, or any other intoxicating liquors.* The Secretary of Defense is authorized to make such regulations as he deems appropriate governing the sale, consumption, possession of, or traffic in, alcoholic beverages to or by members of the armed forces or the National Security Training Corps at or near a camp, station, post, or other places primarily occupied by members of the armed forces or the National Security Training Corps.

Any person who knowingly violates such regulations may be punished by a fine of $1,000 or imprisoned for not more than 12 months or punished under the Uniform Code of Military Justice. . . .

18. *Continued liability for induction of persons now or hereafter deferred.* Persons now or hereafter deferred from induction will remain liable for induction into the armed forces or the National Security Training Corps until they attain the age of 35. . . .

[Another provision removes, until July 31, 1954, the previous 2 per cent limitation of the number of women in the armed forces. That is, voluntary enlistments in the women's services may be accepted without regard to the ratio of women to men in the armed forces.]

UNIVERSAL MILITARY TRAINING

1. *Establishment of Commission and National Security Training Corps.* The [law] . . . provides for the establishment of a National Security Training Commission to be composed of five members. Three members shall be civilians and two shall be active or retired members of the regular components of any of the armed forces. Of the three civilian members, not more than two shall be of the same political party.

The Chairman of the Commission must be a civilian. At such time as the Commission is appointed, a National Security Training Corps is established. . . .

2. *Compensation for Commission.* The [law] . . . provides for a per diem of $50 to be paid to members of the Commission while engaged in the business of the Commission. . . .

3. *General authority of Commission.* The [law] . . . provides that the Commission, subject to the direction of the President, shall exercise general supervision over the training of the National Security Training Corps and further provides that such training shall be basic military training. It authorizes the Commission to establish such policies and standards with respect to the conduct of the training of members of the corps as are necessary to carry out the objectives of the act. The Secretary of

Defense is authorized to designate the military departments to carry out the training. The military departments so designated shall carry out the military training in accordance with the policies and standards established by the Commission. Subject to the approval of the Secretary of Defense, and subject to the policies and standards established by the Commission, the military departments shall determine the type or types of military training to be given to the members of the National Security Training Corps. . . .

    4. *Legislative recommendations.* Not later than four months following the confirmation of members of the Commission, the Commission shall submit to the Congress legislative recommendations which shall include, but not be limited to, a broad outline deemed by the Commission and approved by the Secretary of Defense to be appropriate to assure that the training carried out under the provision of the proposed legislation will be of a military nature.

There is a specific provision . . ., however, stating that the Commission shall not have the authority to prescribe the basic type or types of training to be given members of the Corps. Thus the legislative recommendations will contain language which will grant the Commission authority to assure that the training carried out shall be of a military nature, but the Commission will not submit legislative recommendations prescribing the types of basic military training to be given members of the National Security Training Corps.

In addition, the [law] . . . provides that legislative recommendations with respect to a code of conduct, disability and death benefits, and other benefits and obligations and measures deemed necessary to implement any policies and standards established by the Commission shall be submitted by the Commission for legislative action. . . .

The recommendations must be referred to both Committees on Armed Services, and both committees, not later than the expiration of the first period of 45 calendar days of continuous sessions of Congress following the date on which the recommendations are submitted to the Congress, must report thereon to their respective Houses. . . .

5. *Induction into the National Security Training Corps.* The [law] . . . provides that no person shall be inducted into the National Security Training Corps until after (1) a code of conduct has been enacted and measures providing for disability and death benefits have been enacted into law, (2) that the other legislative recommendations submitted by the Commission have been considered and such recommendations or any portion thereof shall have been enacted with or without amendments into law, and (3) the period of service required of persons who have not attained the nineteenth anniversary of the day of their birth has been reduced or eliminated by the President or by the adoption of a concurrent resolution by the Congress.

Thus, the Congress will have an opportunity to consider and amend all of the recommendations submitted by the Commission, and no person can be inducted into the National Security Training Corps until this has taken place. . . .

6. *Pay of members of the National Security Training Corps.* . . . Members of the National Security Training Corps would be paid $30 per month but . . . their dependents would be entitled to the benefits of the Dependents Assistance Act. . . .

7. *Period of service.* The [law] . . . provides that persons inducted into the National Security Training Corps shall be trained for a period of 6 months. . . .

8. *Age of induction.* At such time as induction into the National Security Training Corps is authorized, all persons thereafter registered who have not been inducted into the armed forces and who have not attained their nineteenth birthday shall be liable for induction into the National Security Training Corps. Since men are required to register at the age of 18, this will permit the induction of men into the National Security Training Corps after they have attained their eighteenth birthday. There will probably be an average period of approximately 3 months elapse between registration, classification, and induction. . . .

9. *Initiating induction into the National Security Training Corps.* Induction into the National Security Training Corps may take place after (1) a code of conduct has been enacted, (2) death and disability benefits for members of the corps have been enacted, (3) the other legislative recommendations sub-

mitted by the Commission have been considered and any portion thereof have been enacted into law, and (4) at such time as the President or the Congress by the adoption of a concurrent resolution has reduced or eliminated the period of service required of persons who have not attained the anniversary of their nineteenth birthday.

Persons who are deferred for any of the reasons provided in the proposed legislation shall not be exempt from their liability for induction into the National Security Training Corps merely because they have passed their nineteenth birthday. . . .

10. *Overseas assignment of members of the National Security Training Corps.* No person inducted into the National Security Training Corps may be assigned for training at any installation outside the continental United States except that residents of the territories and possessions of the United States may be trained in the territory or possession from which they were inducted.

SELECTIVE SERVICE IN HISTORY [2]

The principle of requiring able-bodied men to participate actively in the defense of the nation in time of war dates back almost to the days of primitive society. In the beginning, the family had to stand ready to combat its enemies; families gathered into tribes and finally from tribes into nations to bring greater strength and ability to defend themselves.

In the first chapter of Numbers in the Holy Bible, we are told that Moses and Aaron registered and classified the Jews, placing 603,550 able-bodied men in the fighting class, or as we know it 1-A. The Roman Emperors, under Caesar, drafted men for 10 years of military service, and those conscripts were required to furnish their own equipment.

In America, the recognition of an able-bodied male citizen's obligation for military service is older than the nation itself. The Pilgrims and colonists of those days, if they were to survive,

---

[2] From "Selective Service, Its History and Its Functions," by Colonel Paul G. Armstrong, Illinois State Director, Selective Service System. *State Government*, 23:267-70. December 1950. Reprinted by permission.

had to be in a constant state of preparation. All men in the colonies were obligated to serve in the common defense. The Continental Congress recognized the necessity of defense, and on July 18, 1775, recommended to the inhabitants of the then united English colonies that all able-bodied men between 16 and 50 years of age be formed into companies of militia. Though conscription as we know it now was not actually used at that time, militia groups were formed in the several colonies. In 1776, with the formation of the new republic under the Articles of the Confederation, the central government had the necessary authority to wage a war effectively and successfully.

George Washington, realizing the need for manpower control and volume, proposed to the first Congress a plan which contemplated a registration and classification of the new nation by age and physical fitness and to segregate the fit men between 18 and 25 years of age into tactical units so that they might receive selected training under qualified instructors; the men were to be retained in service as long as might be necessary. Had the Congress authorized this forerunner of selective service, there might have been a resultant shortening of the war but, despite the pleas of Washington, Jefferson, and Madison, it failed to adopt such a law. In 1787, when the Constitution of the United States was adopted, the nation's founders provided that Congress should have power to declare war, to raise and support armies, to provide and maintain a navy, to make rules for the government of the land and naval forces and to provide for the calling of the militia, to execute the laws of the Union, to suppress insurrections, and to repel invasions.

Subsequently, Congress on May 8, 1792, enacted legislation titled "An Act more effectually to provide for the National Defense by establishing a Uniform Militia throughout the United States." Section 1 of the act provided in part "That each and every free able-bodied white male citizen . . . who is or shall be of the age of 18 years shall . . . be enrolled in the militia." A mandatory statute hereby established in the new Federal Government the traditional principle of the citizen's obligation for military service and the government's power to compel such service. This statute remained on the books for more than 111 years.

UNIVERSAL CONSCRIPTION

After the start of the Civil War, the Confederate Congress adopted and passed a Conscription Act which made the Confederate armies more stable than those of the Northern states, which had not established any military policy and did not establish one until the Enrollment Act of 1863 was passed. This [Act of 1863] provided that the draft should be conducted solely by the Federal Government and for three years. Although this was not a good law, even with the amendments made later, it did provide a greater stability to the Northern armies insofar as manpower was concerned.

Brigadier General James Oakes, who administered the Enrollment Act of 1863 in Illinois as assistant provost marshal general, wrote a report of his administration of it. His recommendations and conclusions have served as the starting point for most of the planning for subsequent American mobilization. Probably the greatest value of the report was to teach subsequent planners to avoid the errors inherent in the Enrollment Act. Without question, the greatest success of the operation under the 1940 Act may be attributed in part to the knowledge gained from study of the Oakes report.

The war with Spain in 1898 was fought entirely by voluntary forces, and it was not necessary to provide for compulsory service.

In 1903 the act that had been on the statute books since 1792 was repealed, and the Act of 1903 was passed, clearing the way for a return to colonial tradition and a modernized version of Washington's "peace establishment." This new law defined the militia as consisting of "every able-bodied male citizen . . . and every able-bodied male of foreign birth who has declared his intention to become a citizen, who is more than 18 and less than 45 years of age. . . ." Under this law, the modern National Guard of the United States was organized, and those citizens who were not members of this organized unit were to be known as the reserve militia. The President was empowered to call any part of the militia to active service for a period not to exceed 9 months. . . .

On April 6, 1917, . . . war between the United States and the Imperial German Government . . . was formally declared. Forty days later the Selective Service Act of 1917 was enacted.

Under this law nearly three million men were selected and inducted.

In the years between 1920 and 1940, the General Staff, in accordance with the mandate of an act of June 4, 1920, prepared plans for national defense and the mobilization of the nation's manpower. In 1926 the Joint Army and Navy Selective Service Committee was established and began to function in the preparation and revision of the Selective Service Act, the regulations that would be based thereon, and plans of organization and administration so that the Selective Service System might procure men for the armed forces with a minimum disturbance of the economic and social structure of the nation.

The 76th Congress passed the Selective Training and Service Act of 1940, which became effective September 16, 1940. The system that operated during World War II was the product of the 1917-18 experience plus 14 years of thinking and planning by the members of the Joint Army and Navy Selective Service Committee in collaboration with officers of the National Guard and reserve officers of the army, navy, and marine corps. We were successful in World War II because there was an established military policy. Plans that had been developed by able men, and were ably administered, had been placed in operation almost 15 months prior to the time we actually became involved in war. A million men had been trained and were ready for service; the machinery of selective service was in operation in thousands of communities throughout the United States and its territories. The local boards were manned by patriotic citizens willing to give their time to the nation without compensation or hope of reward. Of the total number of 14.6 million who gained military status, approximately 10 million were inducted through the selective service boards and required a minimum of 30 million classification acts by the local and appeal boards of the nation. . . .

Under the law, although selective service is a federal agency, the governor of a state is the head of the system within his state and is authorized under the law to delegate his authority to a qualified citizen who serves as the state director and who, under the Director of Selective Service, administers the law within his state.

This provision, under which the governor actually is the head of selective service, was placed in the law to correct one of the most serious conditions that existed in the operation of the Enrollment Act during the Civil War. It was intended to insure that the state would be in a position to protect its rights and not permit the national military service to control the induction of citizens within a state into the military forces. It was to insure, instead, a civilian administration, by the state under the governor, although as a federal agency paid by and instructed under laws passed by Congress. . . .

The Act of 1940 was terminated in 1947, and was succeeded by the Office of Selective Service Records.

In the spring of 1948 with unsettled conditions in many parts of the world and with the increasing menace brought about by the evident effort on the part of Soviet Russia to widen and increase its influence over heretofore independent nations of the world, the President of the United States reported to Congress the need for increasing the nation's armed strength. As a result, Congress passed the "Selective Service Act of 1948," for a two-year duration, to provide for the common defense by increasing the strength of the armed forces, including the reserve components thereof, and for other purposes. On June 24, 1948, a new Selective Service System was created, and it followed closely the policies established under the 1940 act.

Under title 1, section 1, paragraph C states: "The Congress further declares that in a free society the obligation and privileges of serving in the armed forces and the reserve components thereof should be shared generally, in accordance with a system of selection which is fair and just, and which is consistent with the maintenance of an effective national economy."

Under this act . . . only a nominal number of men were inducted, and inductions finally were stopped at the end of January 1949. Only registration and classification were continued. . . .

Then in June [1950] . . ., Russia, through its North Korean satellite, moved across the 38th parallel. On June 20, 1950, Congress extended the law until July 9, 1951, and directed that the armed strength be increased.[3] The local boards of the nation,

[3] The law has now been extended to July 1, 1955. See previous selection.—Ed.

although on a part-time basis, had classified hundreds of thousands of citizens into Class 1-A, as available for military service. These classifications could not be reviewed because of the great and immediate need for men for the armed services, as the local boards were called upon immediately for quotas of men for physical examination and subsequent induction. . . .

The value of having the selective service organization on a standby basis was proved by the fact that, when danger again appeared on the horizon and it was necessary to increase the size of the armed forces, this system was prepared, with the local boards still organized all over the nation and the machinery ready to move.

A LONG-RANGE PROGRAM FOR SELECTIVE SERVICE [4]

In the building and maintaining of the armed forces there are many factors to be weighed in the search for a satisfactory program for the procurement of manpower. Numbers are, of course, the usual measure of size, but confusion lurks behind the apparent simplicity of numbers. The numbers of men which must must be procured to maintain a given number in the armed forces are much greater than that number. The numbers in our population tend to promote a philosophy of abundance in our public that is not justified by the size of the manpower pool in the ages best fitted for service in the armed forces.

Age is one of the most important factors in the analysis of manpower for service in the armed forces. The qualities required for service under varied conditions are found to a greater degree in the late teens and the early and middle twenties than any other age. Age combines with many of the factors to be discussed.

One of these is acceptability. Lack of acceptability is responsible for the loss of large numbers of manpower. Standards of acceptability must be sufficiently high to insure the procure-

---

[4] From statement by Major General Lewis B. Hershey, Director of Selective Service, before the Preparedness Subcommittee of the Committee on Armed Services, United States Senate, January 18, 1951. Mimeographed. Selective Service System. Washington, D.C. 1951. Also included, with full discussion, in the Hearings of the Subcommittee on S. 1. Committee on Armed Services, United States Senate, Washington, D.C. 1951. p505-40.

ment of usable men, they must be low enough to use all who can make a contribution to survival. Acceptability decreases with age and with accelerated rapidity once the late twenties have been passed.

The basis of a claim for dependency may be a father, a mother, a sister, a brother, a wife, a child, or a wife and a child or children. If all of these are placed in two classifications they may be referred to as nonfather and father. The numbers with dependents tend to increase as age increases. When an age is reached where this tendency ends the favorable ages for service in the armed forces have been passed.

Occupations and professions possessed by individuals are important in any analysis of manpower. They are found infrequently among the late teens and early twenties. They are found in ever-increasing numbers as the age increases. On the other hand the students preparing for the professions and the apprentices beginning to learn the skills are found almost entirely in the younger age groups.

Veterans at the present time are a most important factor in our manpower problem. . . . The majority of the veterans are above 30 years of age, but a sizable number are under 26 years of age. Veterans, while a separate group, fall into classifications that other individuals do in relation to acceptability, dependency, and occupations or professions. In addition, the length of time served in the armed forces and the circumstances of the service vary greatly among veterans.

The length of the term of service is a factor which means much in the maintenance of the numbers which may be required: 622,000 in 27 months provide the same service as 800,000 in 21 months. The supply of manpower can be divided into two classes according to availability and figuratively designated "capital" and "income." The numbers available at a given time are manpower "capital" while those becoming available each year are manpower "income." We can attain or create a force now from "capital manpower" but we shall have to maintain it through the years from "income manpower."

In the solution of the problem of the use of manpower in the building and the maintenance of our armed forces there are a few requirements which should be used in testing the adequacy of a plan.

First it should be a long-range program. In no other way can the nation be assured that it will have the prescribed numbers in its armed forces at all times. The hurried use of manpower resources in the solution of our problems is expensive in the time and efforts of our people. It is provocative of uncertainty on the part of large segments of our population and does not command the confidence that follows expression of a continuing intent to pursue a constant course of action.

Temporary or short-lived programs for the training of manpower cannot be applied with fairness and justice. It is impossible to institute a plan which would permit of deferments for the purpose of education unless there is assurance that the plan will be continued long enough for those receiving deferments also to meet their service obligations. Otherwise a deferment becomes simply a means of evading service by staying out until the program ends or the law expires.

Second, the plan must be flexible enough to meet the changing requirements for manpower. At the present time the projected size of the armed forces will require service from every acceptable individual in the manpower income as well as those available in the lower ages of the nonveteran groups. Later, if our situation improves, it will be possible to require shorter active service with greater service in the reserve forces. On the other hand, should greater forces be required the plan should readily permit expansion by increasing the length of service, further reducing the rate of rejection, inducting veterans, inducting registrants with dependents, and if necessary successively broadening the liability into the older age groups.

Third, the tax upon the time of the citizen for service with the armed forces should occur at the earliest practicable time. This is to the advantage of the government and of the citizen as well. The youth has more of the qualities required for service in the armed forces than any other age. The responsibilities of family are generally nonexistent in the late teens. Skills have not been acquired, nor has professional or scientific competence been achieved. The earlier this service is completed the less interruption to the productive activities of the citizen. It would seem practicable to limit the service and the active reserve period for the average citizen between the years when he is 18 to 25 inclusive. The individuals above 25 engaged in armed forces activities would be those professionally in the regular forces and those semiprofessionally in the National Guard and active organized reserves.

Fourth, the service required of citizens must be equitable. In the first place, manpower of the proper age and quality is in short supply and the relief of any citizen from the normal term of service will require more service from some other citizen, or the nation will be defended by a smaller number in the armed forces. In the second place, survival is an activity to which all citizens owe a contribution. To relieve any citizen wholly or in part from the obligation he owes will require reasons of the highest importance to the government. Even under these circumstances, unless there is complete understanding of these reasons, the plan is doomed to failure. Certainly wealth or position will not be accepted as reasons for requiring a less arduous contribution in service from a citizen. To what extent the public will accept training for scientific endeavor or the professions as a substitute for or a prelude to service will depend on how well the men to be trained are chosen and how effectively they assimilate and use for the public good the knowledge they achieve.

Fifth, the administration of the program must be simple, it must be understandable, and above all it must have a reputation for integrity. In order to remain simple and understandable there must be a high degree of decentralization and a wide delegation of power. The system of procurement must operate in the communities by citizens of these same communities.

HOW FAIR IS THE DRAFT? [5]

We can't say we haven't been warned. Complacency verging on arrogance cost us irretrievable lives and time during the last

[5] From an article by Stanley Frank, writer. *Nation's Business.* 39:31-3. January 1951. Copyright 1950, by the Chamber of Commerce of the United States. Reprinted by permission.

war and a hang-over of the same attitude is setting us up for another crisis all over again. President Truman had good firepower but erratic aim on October 25 [1950] when he called the high rejection rate of men found physically or mentally unfit in the draft "a disgrace to the richest nation in the world." The President, referring to World War II statistics, mentioned a rejection rate of 34 per cent—actually, it was 35.8 per cent—but newspapers carrying his speech told a more alarming story.

Reports from local selective service boards throughout the country revealed that 45 to 80 per cent of the men called up since Korea had been turned down by the army. The implication was clear: The draft was in trouble. . . .

Something, obviously, is wrong. Americans are the best fed, clothed and housed, the most thoroughly doctored and scrubbed people on the face of the earth. There is a direct correlation between a high standard of living and physical vigor and mental stability, but the figures don't add up. By our own admission, one young man in every three is a pantywaist or a psychoneurotic.

We must be better than the figures say we are. If we were not, we would have been licked decisively in two bloody wars. We are not as good, however, as the [military leaders] . . . in the Pentagon think we are. A military axiom holds that a nation, or a coalition, faces certain defeat when one third of its forces in the field is eliminated by casualties. The United States is undermining its security by eliminating one third of its available manpower before uniforms are issued. That policy inevitably will catch up with us when, for the first time in our history, we and our allies are opposed by an enemy numerically stronger. It will be too late then to correct mistakes. Second chances are buried in the rubble that mounts with the increasing fury of all-out war.

Who says one third of our young men are unfit to serve in the armed forces? The answer will come as a surprise to most citizens. The armed forces, which arbitrarily establish their own criteria, say so. The army, navy, and air force which, like all military organizations from time immemorial, complain—perhaps justifiably—that they do not have enough of everything they need, say they cannot use one youth in every three. And what is the basis for this strange contention?

Now we are getting to the heart of the matter and the answer no longer can remain unchallenged. The armed forces of the United States insist on regarding every recruit as a potential combat man. It is a concept as archaic as a cavalry charge with drawn sabers and as unrealistic as an umbrella in an air raid, yet our military leaders continue to adhere to it despite the experience of disastrous consequences. Their own elaborate tables of organization prove that the idea of training every volunteer and conscript for front-line fighting is utter nonsense.

The old saw to the effect that 20 men are needed behind the guy with the rifle is not a rule of thumb. Less than 5 per cent of all the men in the armed forces in the last war saw, much less engaged, the enemy in combat. No more than 15 per cent ever heard a shot fired in anger. Even in an infantry division, fewer than half the troops are assigned to rifle companies. The overwhelming bulk of men in every army, navy and air force, especially the American, is occupied with logistics and the technical aspects of modern war, a trend highlighted in startling fashion by comparisons of World Wars I and II. The total United States Army mobilized in April 1945 was more than twice as large as that mobilized in November 1918—but the strength of combatant ground forces was just about the same.

Another lucid example of the same sort of thing—but on a lower level—comes from General Mark W. Clark, the Army Field Forces chief. The general has estimated that an infantry division of 19,000 men under the present setup probably would call for 60,000 to handle the rear-area service activities. The Red Army has only 5,000 to 6,000 backers-up per combat division.

What were all noncombatant GIs doing during the last war? They were hauling supplies, driving and maintaining vehicles, handling communications, sorting mail, making propaganda, guarding installations and supply lines, cooking chow, administering liberated and conquered territory, planning future operations and keeping records in triplicate for still others to file. The million and one details that, while not so dangerous, were just as necessary to supply and maintain riflemen, tanks, ships and planes, employed 95 per cent of the men in uniform.

Few of those rear echelon jobs required top physical condition, and every military organization in the world except the United States' has recognized that fact. The United States alone accepts only first-rate physical specimens, regardless of their eventual assignments. The result, of course, is that such men are diverted from the front lines, where strength and stamina are needed, to duties that can be discharged satisfactorily by the majority of men who are rejected.

No other nation is deluded by what Major General Lewis B. Hershey, Director of Selective Service, calls "a philosophy of abundance"—a polite way of saying the United States is dissipating its manpower with an overconfidence that smacks of insolence. Every other country, friendly or hostile, has three to seven classifications for conscripts according to physical capabilities. They operate on the theory that a job can be found in the service for any man of military age who is gainfully employed in civilian life. The United States takes men who qualify only for combat and discards the millions who can be competent clerks, truck drivers, mechanics, guards, cooks and technical specialists.

Despite the manpower shortage, there still is not a general limited-service classification for draftees in the army, the only branch now drawing on selective service to meet its authorized strength. The navy and air force are getting enough volunteers to fill their needs, although they shortly will feel the pinch of expansion. The tragic lessons of the last war have been forgotten or ignored. We were at war for nearly two years in 1943 before all three branches agreed, reluctantly, to accept men who did not measure up to their physical and mental standards for combat. It was a shortsighted policy that eventually cost lives and unquestionably delayed the successful prosecution of the war.

As early as September 1942, the army ground forces were short 330,000 men, the services of supply 34,000, the air force 103,000 and the mushrooming navy was severely strapped. In June 1943, the manpower situation was so acute that 500,000 men were dropped from the proposed strength of the army. Only then did our military authorities scrape the bottom of the barrel —as they condescendingly called it—but it already was too late. Three months after the invasion of Normandy, rear echelons

UNIVERSAL CONSCRIPTION

were combed frantically and their rugged men in desk and administrative jobs were rushed to the front. GIs were sent into combat with insufficient training; a "calculated risk"—a euphemism for lines stretched to the breaking point—led to the Battle of the Bulge and the largest number of casualties suffered by American forces in any ten-day period of the war.

It would be fine if every young American in uniform could tear down a brick wall with his bare hands after a 20-mile march with a full pack. It would be even more wonderful if no young American had to wear a uniform at all, but such wishful thinking is as dangerous as the first hypothesis. We cannot afford the luxury of either one. The facts in the case are uncompromising and inescapable.

To maintain a defense establishment of 3 million men, 800,000 new men a year are needed to fill the gaps left by completed tours of duty. During the 1940s, some 1.2 million men reached the draft age every year. The United States then was cashing in on the prosperity of the 1920s, which, as always is the case in good times, produced a high birth rate. But this year, and every year until 1957—the most critical period of our relations with Russia, according to military and diplomatic authorities—fewer than a million men will turn 18. We now are getting into the depression babies of the 1930s, when the birth rate fell to an all-time low.

You can't beat the percentages. If one third of the million youths reaching military age are rejected, the United States will not have the 800,000 recruits needed every year to keep its armed forces at the minimum level needed for the nation's security—and the situation will get progressively worse, of course. . . .

What is the solution? Reduce the strength of the armed forces? That's unthinkable in the present political climate. Expand the 19 to 26 age limit of the draft? The net will catch only veterans of World War II who already have discharged honorably their obligations to the country. It is unfair to expose these men to double jeopardy. Uprooting them again will dislocate severely the nation's economy, to say nothing of the emotional strains married men and their families will suffer. Lower the draft age to 18? That will solve nothing after the first year.

There is an easy, effective and equitable solution. The chief drain on our military manpower pool is the rejection rate for physical and mental deficiencies. . . . Since the standards are substantially the same as in the last war, it is reasonable to assume that about 35 per cent of the men coming up will be declared unfit again.

We cannot afford to eliminate one young man in every three. We need not lose more than 300,000 men a year if a reform, dictated by logic and necessity, is adopted.

The physical standards for induction must be lowered. It can be done without impairing the efficiency of the armed forces by the simple expedient of junking the outmoded notion that every conscript must qualify for combat.

Dr. Henry H. Kessler, who was in charge of the rehabilitation program at Mare Island in California during the war, believes 75 per cent of the men rejected can be used for general —not limited—service if the present physical standards are lowered.

"It can be accomplished without fuss or bother," Dr. Kessler says, "in six to eight weeks during regular boot training."

Dr. Howard W. Rush, chief of the Convalescent Service during World War II, mentioned on July 22, 1950, some specific jobs industry has found for the physically handicapped. "Dwarfs proved invaluable in the construction of airplane wings; paraplegics produced precision instruments; the blind proved that many assembly lines are operated as well by touch as by sight; the deaf showed that inability to hear can be minimized by written instruction, and cripples of every sort more than pulled their weight."

Look at some of the more common reasons for disqualification the army still is applying in the current draft. A man is rejected if his feet are not good enough for marching. No consideration is given to the proposition that the man can be used in a desk job that involves walking only to the nearest filing cabinet, mess hall and washroom. The minimum height requirement for the armed forces is five feet, two inches and the maximum is six feet six. Lack of height is a definite asset to a mechanic in the cramped quarters of a tank, a jeep motor or the fuselage of a plane. Excessive height can facilitate the handling of supplies in a quartermaster depot.

Men with perforated eardrums are rejected because poison gas is fatal to them. Gas has not been used as a weapon since World War I. Men who cannot see at 20 feet what normal vision sees at 400 feet are rejected. Sounds reasonable until you consider that visibility of 24 inches is all that is required to operate a typewriter.

The thousands of professional athletes who were classified 4-F during the war and continued making muscles provoked so much criticism among servicemen and their families that the army made an official study of such exemptions. It was found that the majority of them were deferred for trick knees.

"Those fellows would be a liability on the battlefield if they threw their knees out of joint," an army spokesman commented. "Suppose they popped a cartilage in the Pentagon?" I asked. The man changed the subject.

The United States would have no manpower crises, no agonizing shortages of combat troops, if an effort were made to use, rather than discard, every youth regardless of physical handicaps. Like all generalizations, this one must be modified. Although spastics and paraplegics can work in offices and release men for more rigorous duty, the problem of transporting and caring for them might tie up more fit personnel than were replaced. Men who must have special diets for organic gastric ailments also might complicate army routine. Severe heart cases and a few other categories would have to be deferred. But as a basic proposition, every man of military age—the one material resource we cannot roll off assembly lines, for all our productive genius—able to live a normal life in civilian society should have a place in the armed forces.

Military people will howl. They will argue that establishing several classifications for physical capabilities demands as many different training programs. So what? Other countries do it. Sure, it means a lot of staff work. So what? For that matter, it is a palpable waste of time and money to give everyone under arms the intense training for combat only 5 per cent needs. Further, setting up limited-service components to take care of supply, housekeeping and bookkeeping chores will enable the brass to train more thoroughly the men who do the actual fighting.

Apart from military expediency, there is an equally strong recommendation for selective service that combines less selectivity with more service. Civilian confidence in the draft as a democratic, impartial process will get a boost.

There will be less uncertainty, less finagling for occupational deferments if every young man knows he has an unpleasant, but necessary, obligation to perform. As General Hershey says, "I haven't seen a draft questionnaire yet in which the guy said he shot people for a living." There will be less griping in the armed forces if everyone knows he is in the same boat with all other members of his generation.

SHOULD SUPERIOR COLLEGE STUDENTS BE DEFERRED? [6]

Yes!

1. The new deferment plan [see footnote below] *offers the best solution for our immediate and long-range needs.* Many people have the idea that college students will not have to serve in the armed forces. This is not true. The new plan merely *defers* their service until they complete college.

The plan is flexible. If the army suddenly needs more men than it had anticipated, the aptitude test "passing" score can be raised. Also, the level of required scholastic achievement in college can be made stiffer. This will make more men available

---

[6] From an article by Herbert L. Marx, Jr., associate editor of *Scholastic Magazines*. *Senior Scholastic.* 58:12-13. April 25, 1951. Reprinted by permission of Scholastic Corporation. This selection debates the wisdom of deferring college students with superior aptitudes or grades from selective service. Such a procedure was recommended by the Selective Service System in early 1951, but local draft boards were given final authority to defer or order the immediate induction of these college students.—Ed.

UNIVERSAL CONSCRIPTION

to the draft without delay. Similarly, if the army's need for draftees decreases, then the standards can be lowered to permit even more students to remain in college.

There are 1,059,000 males enrolled in college. Nearly two thirds of these are not eligible for the draft anyway—because they are veterans, 4-Fs, or are in the Reserve Officers Training Corps (and face active duty upon graduation). Only 370,000 college men are draft eligibles, and of these a sizable number are still under draft age. (Figures are from the United States Office of Education.)

2. We are in the midst of a long-range mobilization program. We cannot afford to disrupt college training of future leaders simply to meet our immediate draft problem.

"If you stop farming," J. R. Killian, Jr., president of Massachusetts Institute of Technology, observes, "people starve, or if you shut down the railroads, the nation's economy grinds to a halt. But if you stop education, people merely remain ignorant and not uncomfortable, and the disastrous effects of the ignorance do not become clear for years. . . . If we prematurely disrupt or seriously curtail our higher education, we could in the end wind up with a disastrous shortage of trained manpower. . . . You can't fight a modern war or maintain a modern peace without highly trained manpower."

Forty years ago we needed one engineer for every 170 industrial workers. Today we need one engineer for every 70 industrial workers. Yet the number of engineering graduates each year is declining—even without draft calls.

3. We need college graduates who have studied in many different fields—not just scientists and doctors. The new deferment plan achieves this objective. It asks only that college men be good students in their fields.

We cannot foretell what fields will become "essential" in th future. Ten years ago, we might have considered a nuclear physicist as a theoretician not essential to the nation's defense. Today's student of Far Eastern languages or of economics may become a highly valued specialist for national defense tomorrow.

By deferring students regardless of what they are studying, we put a greater challenge to them to study as hard and as thoroughly as they possibly can. When they do enter the army for their term of service later on, they will be better prepared for their military duties.

4. *Scholarships can be provided by Uncle Sam to permit needy and deserving students to go to college.* The Trytten Committee [an advisory group of scientists who originally proposed the deferment plan] suggests a "national scholarship program" to give financial aid to boys who show the desire and capacity for college training, but who cannot afford it themselves.

No!

1. *The new deferment plan is totally undemocratic and unfair.* There is no more reason for deferring college students than there is for deferring young men with red hair. An immediate penalty is placed, for example, on the high school graduate who passes up college in order to go to work and help support his family.

Nor does the vague promise of federal scholarship aid help much. For every boy who goes to college there is another one of equal ability who does not and cannot go. The scholarship program, even if Congress approved it, could hardly begin to cover all deserving young men.

And there is no clear assurance that college men will have to serve after graduation. Who can predict with certainty that we will be drafting men in 1953 or 1955? Or, if we will be doing so, why should the noncollege man risk his life . . . now while the college man may do nothing more than serve in a more peaceful post in the future?

2. *Aptitude tests and college grades are not fair measurements to use.* Most educators agree that aptitude tests do little more than measure family, economic, and educational backgrounds. A boy of wealthy parents who attended a good prep school will probably do better than a farmer's son who attended

a poorly equipped high school. But both boys might have equal native intelligence and willingness to learn.

Grades, too, are often meaningless. Some colleges have standards so low that a student can be in the top half of his class and still be no better educated than many high school seniors in a good central high school.

3. *The policy will work a hardship on many college students.* The new deferment plan will make many sincere, patriotic college students the object of derision as "draft evaders." They will be accused of finding a "soft berth"—which they actually did not seek.

Likewise, students who fail the aptitude test, have low grades, and are drafted will be looked upon as "stupid" by both their classmates and their army buddies. This, of course, is totally unfair.

4. *There are several good alternative plans.* It is true that we do not want to close our colleges, nor do we wish to deprive the armed services of the men they need. But there are many solutions other than the undemocratic student deferment plan.

One, for example, is put forward by James B. Conant, president of Harvard and a member of the Committee for the Present Danger. It calls for universal military service of practically all young men at age 18 for two years. After this service, a young man would be free to go to college, start work, or do whatever he wishes—along with thousands of others his own age. This would have a bad effect on colleges only for a short period, until the first men ended their two-year service and started college.[7]

Another plan calls for drafting all eligible young men and then sending some of them to college at government expense, training them in jobs which would be of value in our defense effort.

Either of these plans, or any of a number of others which have been put forward, would be far more in keeping with our

---

[7] See article by Dr. Conant in following section.—Ed.

democratic traditions than the inequitable deferment of the brighter college students.

ROLE OF THE CONSCIENTIOUS OBJECTOR [8]

It is a part of a great American tradition that the sincere conscientious objector to war shall not be asked to violate his conscience and do military duty. This was so in the War of 1812. It was so in the Civil War. It was so in World War I and . . . in World War II. . . .

The conscientious objection that has been recognized is conscientious objection based on religious grounds. What is called "conscientious" objection may be based on philosophical, humanitarian, economic, or political grounds. None of these has been regarded as a sufficient basis for substituting noncombatant or nonmilitary service in whatever form for combatant service. Protest against the administration of the conscientious-objector clause of the 1940 [selective service] law was based frequently on the denial of cases involving objection based on nonreligious grounds. This criticism was directed against administrative authorities who were obeying the law. This was energy, if it was to do any good in the situation, that should have been directed to the Congress for an amendment to the law itself.

The reason for the exemption from military duty of religious conscientious objectors and the refusal to exempt others has not . . . been expressed in official documents. But the point seems clear enough. If one feels that the high God has placed upon him a duty clearly and specifically, and the failure to perform it or go contrary to it means the loss of God's love or the loss of one's soul eternally, then it is easy to understand, come what will, that the sincere and conscientious man will follow God's will. . . . He will obey God rather than man, whatever the punishment or sacrifice or denials here, because of a greater eternal future. . . .

[8] From *Universal Military Training,* by Edward A. Fitzpatrick, president, Mount Mary College for Women. McGraw-Hill Book Company, Inc. 1945. p292-316. Reprinted by permission.

There is no necessary connection between the truth and the sincerity of conscientious objection on religious grounds. The reasoning may be "silly," but for the objector it is built upon a rock. . . . The voice that he hears is to him God's word and that is enough.

One of the great problems in recognizing conscientious objection to war is to distinguish between the sincere objector and the pseudo objector. . . . The effort to make this determination makes investigations, interviews, and inquiries that are irritating to the bona fide objector necessary. But there is no certain unmistakable mark of the objector, particularly of the individual objector who is not a member of a church. We know from experience of all wars that cowards and slackers and the fearful have attempted to cloak themselves in the protective garments of conscientious objection. . . .

In the Civil War we recognized members of religious denominations who were prohibited by the rules and articles of faith from bearing arms. . . . [In World War I] the only form of conscientious objection recognized . . . was conscientious objection of members of a well-recognized religious organization or sect whose creed of principles forbade participation in war in any form and whose personal convictions were in accord with the creed. Persons who were available for military service and who had conscientious objection to war were inducted into the army and assigned to do noncombatant service, as defined by the President, in the Medical Corps, the Engineering Corps, and the Quartermaster Corps. The army itself, having these men under its jurisdiction, extended the conception of conscientious objection in accordance with an order of the President to include all persons who conscientiously objected to war on *any* grounds. Numbers of these persons were given what is known as "farm furloughs" or reconstruction work in France. In this, undoubtedly, is the germ of the idea of "civilian work of national importance," but it was never developed [during World War I]. . . .

The War Department proposal of 1940 was the exact proposal of 1917. There had been no development nor a better understanding of the problem. Those opposing the statute or wanting a change of the conscientious-objection provision were responsible for the changes that were made. They worked out with and for the congressional committees the new form. It recognized two forms of conscientious objection—one, which permitted a noncombatant service in the armed forces, and another, which did not require any direct military service or service under military control, but did require that the objector be assigned to work of national importance under civilian direction. The great advance in this field in the administration of the law was the progressive improvement in the character of the work of national importance to which this second group was assigned. . . .

In World War II, the conception of conscientious objection was extended so as not to be restricted to the historical peace churches or to churches forbidding war but was extended to include persons whose conscientious objection was based on religious training and belief. . . .

The American tradition on conscientious objection includes at the present time the following elements:

1. The acceptance of conscientious objection to war, based on religious grounds, as a fact in human experience.

2. The exemption of sincere conscientious objectors on religious grounds from combatant military duty.

3. The requirement that conscientious objectors shall render as nearly equivalent a service as possible.

4. The recognition of two types of service to be rendered by conscientious objectors: (1) noncombatant service, such as service in the medical corps, and (2) civilian work of national importance, such as forest-fire fighting, human guinea pigs in scientific experiment, care of the insane, and the like.

UNIVERSAL MILITARY TRAINING AND SERVICE

EDITOR'S INTRODUCTION

The necessity for some form of compulsory military service in time of national emergency or war for at least some young men is almost universally accepted in the United States. Selective service was debated bitterly prior to our entry into World War II. When the call for selective service legislation was renewed after the war in 1948, it again met opposition, but not nearly so strong. Today, however, there is little or no opposition—in Congress or elsewhere—to the basic principle of involuntary military service for physically fit young men.

Such unanimity does not apply, however, to a program for peacetime universal military training—short periods of preparation for possible future military duty. In June 1951, Congress approved the principle of UMT, but left for a later time further debate on its possible inauguration.

Opposition to UMT comes from two groups: (1) those who believe it unnecessary, unsound, or evil—or a combination of these; and (2) those who believe that UMT is inadequate for the task of supplying military manpower.

Many of the people in the latter group favor, instead, universal military service—that is, required service for *all* young men directly in the armed forces.

This section deals both with the pros and cons of UMT and with opposing views on a proposal for UMS made by Dr. James Bryant Conant. In addition, the section includes the first of three articles in this volume on British experience in manpower controls.

AN OUTLINE OF UMT'S MERITS [1]

1. Universal military training is needed to provide future trained reserves for the armed services. . . . National defense

[1] From *Universal Military Training and the Problem of Military Manpower*, by S. Arthur Devan, analyst on national defense. Public Affairs Bulletin No. 90. Library of Congress. Legislative Reference Service. Washington, D.C. 1951. p47-54. Reprinted by permission.

rests in the last analysis on manpower. Military men have always known this, and our chief military leaders have testified to it again and again, but there has been a cherished tendency in the mind of a large section of the public to feel that now we have airplanes and atomic bombs and other forms of mechanized warfare, we do not need men, or at any rate not in very large numbers. [Former] Secretary [of Defense James] Forrestal replied to this mode of thinking by saying in 1948: "The comfortable assurance of a push-button war is an illusion. The enormous complication of the machinery of total warfare of today rests upon manpower—not in mass, but diffused through thousands of specialities."

The events of Korea have brought this fact home to us very clearly. We have had complete domination of the skies, and eventually we have succeeded in bringing superior weapons on the scene, but up to the [spring of 1951 we had] . . . not succeeded in overcoming the onrush of numerically superior enemy ground forces, described by General MacArthur as "a fanatical foe, well trained, expertly directed and heavily armed."

If future developments should require us to conduct operations, not only in Korea, but in Europe and in the Near East, and in Southeastern Asia, and elsewhere and at the same time to defend ourselves here at home—any or all of which contingencies may happen—we shall need very large forces.

No one believes that we shall have time to train these forces after the war begins. We had years for this in both the world wars, but now we shall need to be able to effect a very swift mobilization. Unless we are to maintain standing forces of monstrous size, which would cripple our economy and do us harm in other ways as well, there is only one answer to the problem: it is to have ready a reservoir of trained citizens who may be called upon.

We have been building up our reserves in recent years, an increase from 435,000 to 834,000 from 1948 to 1950. This increase is due largely to reserve enlistments of patriotic veterans of World War II. The number of these veterans who are capable of service is decreasing year by year, due to age, physical condition, family responsibilities and the like; in any case they should not have to serve in another war while there are millions of younger men who have never done their part.

UMT will provide an annual flow into the National Guard and the various reserve components of the forces of perhaps 800,000 men a year. All of them will have had basic military training, all of them will have had unit training, many of them will have had specialized training of one kind or another, many will have had officer training in some branch of the service. With very little more training—perhaps only two months in many cases—they will, in the opinion of General Omar Bradley, be prepared to be committed to combat. During the recent war when we got down to "scraping the bottom of the barrel" in our manpower, we had to commit men to battle with only a few weeks of training. They made inferior soldiers and many more were killed and wounded than would have been the case had they been properly prepared. . . .

If there is a global war—a possibility which we have to envisage—our chief potential enemy has in being at least 175 divisions, with a reserve of (it is said) 300 more divisions. The satellite countries in addition are supposed to be able to put armies of a million men in the field, without counting China. If we do have to contend with these hordes we shall not only require the most advanced technical weapons, ground, air and sea, but considerable bodies of trained and disciplined men who know how to use them. If we do not have these men, our cause will be hopeless.

2. Universal military training will further the cause of peace and decrease the liability of war. . . .

Dr. Karl T. Compton, of the Massachusetts Institute of Technology, pointed out that captured documents show "Hitler embarked on his aggressive moves because his analysis of the world situation had convinced him that the democratic countries were too weak, too pacifist, and too 'soft' to oppose him, and that before the democracies could have become strong enough to oppose him, he would have reached an impregnable position." Dr. Compton repeated [to Congress in 1950] statements he made two years earlier, feeling that they have even greater force [at present]:

I personally believe that the world would be a more peaceful place and the United Nations would have made greater progress toward their objective . . . if universal military training had been adopted in 1945, when there were strong arguments for it on the basis that we should maintain a strong military posture until the full objective of World War II had been secured. Then again I believe that it would have been advantageous if we could have enacted universal military training legislation a year ago. Now we still have another chance. But in each of these times the need has been more urgent and obvious than before. It certainly seems to me therefore that we should not again allow the lapse of another year before tackling this problem courageously and effectively.

3. Universal military training is needed to assure our friends and allies as well as our potential enemies that we mean business. The countries of Western Europe particularly, whose support means everything to us, are still doubtful if we aim to do more than fight the Communists to the last drop of French blood. They hesitate to go the whole way with us if it means simply that we will send over a few airplanes to bomb their cities after the unopposed Russian ground forces have forced their way into them.

4. Universal military training will not only save time in another possible war, but will save lives. All military leaders, from Eisenhower and Marshall down to the last second lieutenant who fought in the late war, agree that we have had great numbers of unnecessary casualties through insufficient training. Eisenhower says, "I should say that the trained combat soldier has at least three times the chances of the untrained to live to become a veteran." . . . The Disabled American Veterans, at every one of their conventions, have emphasized this point, and their experience would seem to enable them to speak with authority.

5. . . . If an emergency comes, men in service will be far more likely to find themselves in the places for which they are fitted. [At recent Congressional hearings it was pointed out]. . . :

> In the emergency of converting ourselves to a wartime footing, we have always, due to the waste of haste, improperly used the talents and capabilities of our citizen soldiers. UMT would correct this. . . . We would obtain the proper classification of every trainee citizen within the nation.

6. Universal military training will result in personality gains for the trainees. Reasonable discipline, physical examinations discovering early remediable ailments, educational opportunities, the experience of meeting with other Americans from all over the country, increased sense of responsibility, in many cases training in technical skills which can be used in civil life, a sense of citizenship and belonging, a realization that the country has a right to demand something in return for what it has given him, and many other elements of maturity will be brought to thousands of young men who need just these things. . . .

7. Universal military training is essentially the democratic way to meet the problem. It is a sharing of the burden of defense that falls upon all alike—the privileged and the poor. No one can escape it because of means or influence; nor is any one forced into the military because of his inferior economic position, as has too often been the case in the past. Even now, with the operation of selective service, there are complaints arising over the country because, while few are being drafted, one boy will be taken from a neighborhood, while his companions of the same age and position are entirely free to go their ways. Under UMT all will be trained, and trained alike. If an emergency arises, all may be called and called alike.

8. Universal military training will aid in the problem of civil defense. Only now is the country becoming conscious that we too may be bombed. . . . In the past, when disasters have occurred, the militarily trained young men, veterans, have often been the first on the scene. They are used to emergency measures, to quick common action, to leadership and response. In our coming civil defense set-up, it will be of inestimable value to have . . . citizens who know how to act in an emergency.

A PROGRAM FOR NATIONAL SECURITY [2]

After nearly six months of the most intensive study, the members of this [President's Advisory] Commission [on Uni-

[2] From report of the President's Advisory Commission on Universal Training. Superintendent of Documents. Washington, D.C. 1947. p89-95.
This nine-man commission was headed by Dr. Karl T. Compton, now chairman of the Corporation of Massachusetts Institute of Technology. Though not acted

versal Training] have arrived at the unanimous conclusion that universal training is an essential element in an integrated program of national security intended to safeguard the United States and to enable us to fulfill our responsibilities to the cause of world peace and the success of the United Nations.

Our conviction stems from the following basic beliefs:

1. One of the deterrents to the effectiveness of the United Nations is the belief of other nations that we are stripping ourselves of the strength necessary to support our moral leadership and are thus encouraging powers that may not share our peaceful aims to plan campaigns of aggression. We believe that the adoption of universal training would reassure the peace-loving countries of the world and enhance the influence and authority of the United Nations.

2. Universal training offers the only method through which we could insure a sufficient number and dispersal of trained military manpower without overburdening the country's economy through the maintenance of a huge standing army, navy, air force, and marine corps.

3. The addition of the atomic bomb to the incalculable horrors of modern war has eliminated the concept of zones of safety in any future attack on this country. By making war universal, devastating, and immediate in its impact, new developments in warfare have created a need for trained men in every city and town—men who would be available at once in an emergency.

We do not wish, however, to exaggerate the benefits that would be derived from the establishment of a universal training program. It offers no cheap or easy ticket to security. Only when combined with the other elements that enter into a balanced security system would it provide the measure of strength necessary to deter an aggressor from taking up arms against us or from violating the rights of less powerful nations. . . .

We have given careful attention to the argument most frequently put forward against the adoption of a universal training program; namely, that the development of the atomic bomb and

---

on by Congress, this report is such a comprehensive study and endorsement of UMT that it is still used as a basic source by UMT proponents.—Ed.

UNIVERSAL CONSCRIPTION

other instruments of mass destruction has eliminated the need for mass military forces in wartime. We reject this conclusion because our analysis of the possible types and conditions of future warfare convinces us that increased, rather than decreased, numbers of trained troops would be quickly required for home defense, for effective counterattack, and for complete victory.

Specifically, we believe that a universal training program would provide the following benefits:

1. It would shorten the time in which our effective fighting force could be mobilized in case of war.

2. It would give our young men the essentials of military training that would be the basic prerequisites for technical, specialized, or unit training in an emergency; and training saves lives.

3. It would make possible an effective National Guard and organized army, navy, air, and marine reserves capable of rapid absorption into the professional military establishment in time of war.

4. It would improve the efficiency, quality, and alertness of the regular forces in peacetime.

5. It would help produce qualified reserve officers in numbers that would assist in meeting the officer requirements of the regular services and the civilian components and to staff the forces needed after M-day in any future crisis.

6. It would present additional opportunities for inculcating spiritual and moral ideals in support of the American democracy.

7. It would establish a pool of young, physically fit, and trained reserves who could be mobilized if a future crisis arose.

8. It would provide a large trained group in every community capable of withstanding and dealing with the problems of civilian defense and mass disaster resulting from severe bombing attacks.

9. It would provide a mechanism that could be converted immediately into a wartime selective service system, and it would make possible a continuous inventory of military skills, aptitudes, and leadership qualities that could be used advantageously in making military assignments should war come.

10. It would help to channel qualified young men into programs of scientific and vocational training in fields important to national defense.

11. It would bring together young Americans from all parts of the nation to share a common experience and to fulfill a common obligation to their country, thus contributing to national unity, the foundation of our security.

12. It would give greater military strength at less cost than would be provided by exclusive reliance on a large standing military force, since it would be impossible to obtain enough volunteers for the professional force required for adequate defense and since the cost would overburden the national economy even if such a force could be raised.

In submitting a training program intended to achieve these military benefits, we have been mindful of the need for integrating into the program, without sacrificing its essential military objectives, the maximum advantages to health, education, character development, and training for citizenship. We recognize that there are definite limits to the nonmilitary benefits that can be obtained, and we do not present these as in any way a justification for the adoption of a program that must be considered solely on the basis of its contribution to world peace and national security.

The program herein recommended reduces insofar as possible the disruption of normal community and family life, which inevitably attends the calling of young men from their homes in the national interest. We have endeavored to take realistic account of the losses the youth and society would suffer both economically and educationally if the training period were too long, and of the danger that it might be worthless for military purposes if it were too short.

On the basis of all these considerations, we recommend that it be made the obligation of every young man upon reaching the age of 18, or upon completing or leaving high school, whichever is later, to undergo a period of training that would fit him for service to the nation in any future emergency. This period should generally be divided into two parts. The first would be 6 months of basic training in camps or aboard ship. The second would include a number of alternative programs or options, one of which would have to be chosen on completion of the basic training.

The general aim of these options would be (1) to organize men into units, such as those of the National Guard or the reserve components, in which they could keep their basic training up to date, move on to advanced and group training, and be available for effective use in time of war, and (2) to give advanced education or training to those who are qualified for and desire to take such training, including training that would provide a steady stream of young officers. For the most part these options could be performed in connection with, or at the same time as, the pursuit of any occupation in civilian life or of further education.

Six months of basic training is regarded by the Commission as an indispensable foundation without which the whole structure would be of no military utility. It is recognized that entrance into this part of the program will come at an age when most young men are moving from high school to college or are entering upon a vocation. Inevitably, the necessity for spending 6 months in full-time military training will involve some interference with these activities. . . .

We believe that this situation can be handled best by establishing May 1 and November 1 of each year as the dates on which young men would come into the program.

We recommend that the entire training program be placed under the general control and direction of a commission of three members, reporting directly to the President, and composed of two civilians and one military representative. In suggesting that the commission have a civilian majority, we have been guided by our deep conviction that this undertaking must be a civilian effort resting on the understanding, interest, and support of the American people, and surrounded by all the safeguards that the civilian community would wish.

In furtherance of this underlying principle, we also recommend that there be a general advisory board, representative of the public and including leaders in the fields of recreation, religion, education, and health, as well as local civilian advisory committees to each camp commander and a corps of full-time civilian inspectors whose function it would be to see that effective, democratic training is provided in all training establishments in accordance with the policies enunciated by the commission.

We are convinced that it is entirely possible to provide for American youth a wholesome, moral, and religious environment in training camps. . . . We have attempted to evaluate all factors of importance to our security and the maintenance of world peace. Everything points inescapably to the conclusion that there is no real security for this country or any country unless war is abolished through establishment of the reign of law among nations.

We recommend the adoption of universal training because we are convinced that weakness on our part not only involves our country in grave risks but also weakens the United Nations, on which rest our hopes for lasting peace. A weak and irresolute America is an invitation to failure. A strong and resolute America is the best guarantee for our safety and for the success of the United Nations.

NECESSITY—THE BASIC REASON FOR UMT [3]

Many arguments have been advanced for universal military training . . . but all those that have any validity reduce themselves to a single word—necessity. For today's children are being brought up in a far less kindly world than that of their fathers. In the 1930s, to be sure, there was the menace of Hitler's Germany beyond one ocean, the rising tide of Japanese aggression beyond the other. But both were far away; the Japanese were so deeply involved in China that even the best-informed opinion doubted whether they would ever get out, and Nazi Germany was encircled by a combination of forces in the hands of the sea powers of Western Europe and the young democracies east of her. It was possible to believe that neither

[3] From "Should We Have Universal Military Training?" by Fletcher Pratt, military affairs writer and member of the U. S. Naval Institute. *Parents' Magazine*. 26:26+. January 1951. Reprinted by permission.

of the avowed aggressors would ever be in a position dangerous to America, and most people did so believe. The Neutrality Act, which prohibited even the sale of arms to warring nations, was on the books.

Today there are only two great powers in the world, and the other one has pronounced its distaste of every ideal we hold, in unmistakable terms. The Russian Communists have made no secret of their conviction that unless their system embraces the entire world, it cannot exist at all. By their actions they have demonstrated that unless the rest of the world accepts that system voluntarily, they propose to make it do so by force. . . .

What makes this dangerous is the formidable armament in the hands of these aggressive fanatics. They have the largest army the world has seen; the largest air force in existence; and their whole economy is arranged around the idea of keeping civilian life at the bare subsistence level in order more effectively to prepare the state for war. We may not like this idea, but it is one of the fundamental facts of our generation.

What can we do about it? We can give up, of course, in which case there would be no necessity for UMT or any other form of defensive preparation. But unless we choose to do that, I do not see how we can avoid preparing in every possible way for defense. And this does not merely mean building airplanes and adding to our stockpile of atom bombs. The Russians have atom bombs too; and the idea that they can be discouraged in their intentions by the threat or the actuality of this weapon is a futile dream. They have known about it for years, their industry has been dispersed in anticipation of it, they have persisted in their aggressions in the face of the fact that we have it. Moreover, the fighting in Korea has shown that an aggressor can carry out his military intentions in spite of the possibility of any kind of bombing.

It has also shown something else far more ominous—that mere technological superiority is not enough in the face of such vastly superior numbers as the Communists are able to deploy; and, in addition, that if you are going to count on technological superiority, you had better be sure you have it. The qualities of the Russian-made tanks and artillery in Korea came as a nasty surprise to many Americans, even to many Americans in the armed services. We cannot count on defending ourselves against them merely through the number and superiority of our machines.

Nor can we count on the two years of breathing time we had to prepare our defenses in World War II. Hitler and the Japanese both began by imagining they could keep us out of the struggle and addressing themselves to preliminary objectives. The Russians are under no such illusions; they have named us their Public Enemy Number One. Even if they must first take Western Europe, their objective will lie in this country. And if they do take Western Europe, it may be too late. They have no lack of manpower and under their slave system the industrial resources of the Continent would be mobilized against us.

This is perhaps a side issue to the question of UMT. The main fact, the inescapable fact, is that in the event of Russian attack, nothing can save us but having large numbers of men immediately available for the military services. And immediately does not mean within two years or even one year. It means men ready to be organized into units and to go into action within weeks, or at most a couple of months.

These men are not now available, nor are they likely to be unless UMT—or a draft so extensive that it amounts to the same thing—is adopted.

Not only is there every prospect that once war begins there will not be time to train such citizen armies as fought the last two conflicts, but the amount of training those armies received will certainly be utterly insufficient for World War III. This is, indeed, the key fact of the whole situation.

The point is that modern war, by land, sea and air, has become a complex and highly skilled profession. Its technological aspect has advanced farther since 1945 than it did in the twenty years between the two earlier wars. The modern infantryman is required to have a thorough familiarity with at least three weapons that existed only in the experimental stage in 1945, besides knowing all the 1945 soldier had to know about the older weapons and about such purely tactical matters as scouting, patroling, camouflage and communications. More new weapons are coming.

The case is even more pronounced with regard to weapons of the sea and air. With two thirds of our fleet in mothballs, there is, nevertheless, an acute shortage of radar technicians in the navy at the present time; there is a shortage of trained sonar men. Nor can the required skills be supplied from civilian life.

Most of the techniques that are needed by the armed services do not occur in civilian life—a knowledge of how to operate a bazooka, for instance. The men who learned these techniques in the last war have been shoved back into ignorance by the continuing development of new and more complex development of new and more complex weapons. The year that it took to train an efficient soldier or sailor for World War II is nowhere near enough today. Indeed, in the matter of radar men, naval officers complain that a full three-year enlistment is barely enough for the job.

Now, UMT will not give us all the technical specialists we need right off the bat. But it will provide us with a reserve of men who have basic background upon which technical specialization can be imposed. It will provide us with trained infantrymen. It will provide a nucleus of young men who have been tested for qualities of leadership—always the most desirable and difficult thing to find in any group.

Granted that UMT will interfere with their education for the pursuits of peace. Granted that it will interfere with their home life. The domination of the Soviet slave masters would interfere a lot more, not only with our children, but our children's children for many years to come.

AN OUTLINE OF UMT'S FALLACIES [4]

1. Universal military training is not needed, because the wars of the future will not require extensive manpower. The

[4] From *Universal Military Training and the Problem of Military Manpower,* by S. Arthur Devan, analyst on national defense. Public Affairs Bulletin No. 90. Library of Congress. Legislative Reference Service. Washington, D.C. 1951. p55-60. Reprinted by permission.

day of mass armies is past. Increasingly war has become mechanized, and will be more so in the future. It is our scientific research, our industrial output, and our new inventions which will determine the issue.

Particularly is this true with regard to the new factor of air power. Even in [World War II] . . . air power did not come into its own as it will in the future. All victorious warfare must be geared to one primary force. We do not even need what are called "balanced forces," and the land-sea-air team of the recent war is already outmoded. Air power is decisive. It has acquired the range to strike at any target on the face of the earth from its home base and to accept battle anywhere regardless of distance. "Our strategy," says [Alexander P. De] Seversky, "must again look to the classic principle of a single invincible force in the dominant medium. We must prepare to sweep the enemy out of the skies and take complete mastery of the air." Even overseas bases are no longer needed because global command of the air can be exercised, with our long-range bombers, directly from the American continent.

Our long-range bombers with their retaliatory threat are the only reason Russia has not already ventured into open aggressive war. B-36 and even more powerful air units which will be developed in the future are capable of carrying atomic bombs and destroying cities within a few hours after any overt act of war. If, even after such retaliation, a war does develop, it will inevitably be decided by our strategic bombing power; that is, our power to destroy the sources of war production which make the carrying on of war by the enemy possible, and at the same time to destroy the morale of the enemy's civil population. Neither Russia nor any other nation could stand up under this kind of air warfare.

We cannot expect to cope with Russia by land armies, nor will Soviet Russia ever [says Seversky] "be deterred from armed aggression and expansionist aims by universal military training in the U.S.A. and the resurgence of armed divisions in West Europe. These things mean land warfare in which Soviet Russia holds the trump cards. As for sea warfare, Russia has no navy and fears no navy."

Obviously there is then no case for building up large trained reserves for land and sea duty. It is a waste of effort, money, and human life. A comparatively small air force can finish any war by bombing the strategic sources from which the enemy draws his power to make war. That this does not seem to have worked out quite smoothly in the Korean war is wholly irrelevant because that is merely a localized surface contest, and not a war between great powers located on different continents.

2. The actual military training to be given under the UMT program will not be efficient. Soldiers cannot be made by six months in camp. The public is being misled into thinking the training gains will be more effective militarily than is actually the case.

3. The cost of universal military training will be exorbitant. Estimates presented now are unrealistic. This will be a long-time program, and will grow year by year. New stations will have to be built. There will be clamor for more pay, allowance for dependents, subsidies for education and the like. The annual cost may well run up to three, four or five billion dollars. . . . The money would better be spent for public health, education or scientific research.

4. Additional sums will have to be spent for equipment, arms, stockpiling, and ships for transport if there is to be realistic readiness for possible overseas warfare. All this will add up to a vastly expensive program with only a few half-trained soldiers to show for it, and this will have to be repeated year after year.

5. The existence of universal military training will tend to lull the country into a false sense of security, to the neglect of other essential lines of national defense—a kind of Maginot-Line complex. The military leaders and Congress will simply fall back upon the fact that we have an adequate reserve, [just] as in the days before World War II great reliance was placed on the fact that the French army had four or five million trained men in its reserves. "The great expense of any such training program, its probable concentration in training large numbers

of men in methods certain to be obsolete before the next war, and the resultant overemphasis on the creation of a large semi-trained reserve might—and probably would—hamper the development of far more important security measures, an adequate intelligence system, a comprehensive research program, industrial mobilization, finely trained services of professional soldiers, sailors and airmen ready for instant action, and capable leaders" [according to military analyst Hanson W. Baldwin].

6. Universal military training will have an adverse effect on the economic life of the country by withdrawing some 800,000 young men from the labor force of the nation for six months. This withdrawal will come just at the time when these young men will be finishing high school, and should be establishing themselves in regular employment. It will delay their productive efficiency. It may well have the effect of delaying marriages and lowering the birth rate.

7. Universal military training will have an even more deleterious effect on the personality of the coming generations. It means regimentation, which is abhorrent to the American genius. It means militarization of the mind and outlook, and all the promised educational procedures, being directed by military men, are more likely to promote militarism than to develop the individual in useful ways. Even worse are the direct moral effects. It will put these young men in an atmosphere where [as one witness testified before Congress], "men turn to lust and liquor. And when those releases are not available, latent tendencies to homosexuality assert themselves." . . .

8. Universal military training will seriously hamper American education. Withdrawing young men at the age of 18 will interrupt college plans. When the period is over, the desire to go on to college will have been lost, the minds of the trainees dulled, their habits of study diverted, and they will find college work more difficult than would otherwise be the case. Moreover, the Reserve Officer Training Corps features would be clamped down even on colleges which do not wish to the ROTC because trainees going on to college would have to take ROTC. Moreover, the educational features of the program would be likely

to entice teachers away from the colleges, due to higher salaries which the government could afford to pay, and there is already a teacher shortage. So far as educational courses are to be given under UMT itself, the educational value of UMT would probably be something like the educational value of the army and navy. For most soldiers and sailors it was a joke. Their principal education has been in washing dishes, laundering the captain's blouse, or chipping paint.

9. Universal military training will have a disastrous international effect. It will be like telling the world that the United States no longer expects peace or believes in peace. Already the suspicion is widespread over the world, assiduously cultivated by Communist propaganda, that we are an imperialistic power, seeking domination and war. The word that the United States has adopted UMT will give color to all these accusations. It will be more difficult for us to talk peace, with this warlike gesture fresh in people's minds. Especially this will be true in Asia. "We need the Asian peoples [said author Pearl S. Buck in 1948]. We need their good will, their trust and their support. Today they are looking with dread and resentment upon the militarization of the United States. They are giving much thought to what they are going to do about us, and how they are going to withstand us, for they take no stock in our talk of defense against aggression. They see us as the aggressor of tomorrow. They have had their fill of white men coming as aggressors. . . . If we start universal military training they believe, they see, they think already, that we are starting down the bloody European decline."

10. Approaching the problem from another angle and not seeking to question UMT on technical grounds, but referring the whole matter to their Christian philosophy of life, UMT is regarded as wrong by certain religious pacifist groups, which do not feel that political and military circumstances should be permitted to "alter the unchanging commandments of Jesus Christ as we have read them in the New Testament." Accordingly these minority religious groups are "opposed to both selective service

and universal military training as un-Christian and dangerous in the light of history."

JEOPARDIZING THE NATIONAL WELFARE [5]

The passage of a universal military training and service law would seriously jeopardize the national welfare. It would divide the nation by creating the suspicion that an emergency was being used by the military as an opportunity to secure permanent conscription which, in peacetime, Congress and the people have not been willing to accept.

Millions of Americans view with deep concern efforts to fasten upon our country a permanent conscription system on the European pattern. They have again and again acceded in time of crisis to emergency draft legislation, but they are alarmed at proposals to impose on future generations the heart of the Prussian system of militarism.

Universal military service would weaken as well as divide the nation. It would take men away from where they are essential and put them where they are useless. [Selective Service Director] General Hershey's statement is an illustration of the danger to which a democracy may succumb if it turns over every citizen to the military. He said: "We've gotten too big and are thinking in terms of letting a man in a war do what he can do best. That's a false philosophy. . . . Now my idea is that . . . many people are going to have to be made into fighters though their best qualifications are in other fields."

This is a false philosophy of security which would injure the nation's science, education, and health. Because the armed forces in the last war put a college generation of scientific personnel into army camps, there is an estimated shortage of about 17,000 research scientists and 150,000 top technical men. We are told that because of this false philosophy only 166 Americans received doctorates in bacteriology, only 278 in mathematics, and only 416 in physics in the three years from 1946 through 1948.

[5] From *The Cost of Universal Military Service*, by the National Council Against Conscription. Washington, D.C. 1951. p 1-5. Reprinted by permission.

UNIVERSAL CONSCRIPTION

A postwar Report to the President on Medical Research submitted by John R. Steelman, Chairman of the President's Scientific Research Board, described how "the war disrupted the training of research scientists and depleted the faculties of medical schools to a critical extent." The report added: "The effect of the war on medical investigators will still be felt for some years. The interruption of training, the loss of yearly recruitment of young undergraduate students, can be overcome only gradually.". . .

The nation's schools have a critical shortage of teachers. During the last war 85,000 teachers were taken by the armed forces, most of whom never returned to their profession. At the same time only a trickle of teachers was graduated from the nation's colleges, and the supply stayed below normal for several years, according to the United States Office of Education.

If the nation were to adopt universal military training and service, the supply of those taking teacher training woud be stopped. As the New York *Times* education editor has indicated: "It is important, however, to remember that the nation's schools are vitally important at all times, and are even more essential during times of stress. Education is our best bulwark against the spread of communism."

During the first years of any program of universal military service, when all male high school graduates would be drafted . . . the nation's colleges would suffer so drastically in enrollment that many of them could continue functioning only with a costly government subsidy that might result in a measure of government control. No emergency program should be devised so hastily as to jeopardize the educational system upon which America must rely both in war and peace.

The nation's educational standards would suffer in other ways. Not only would the education of boys be interrupted by universal military service, but many would, after several years of military life, want to marry, raise families and earn the necessary support for those families. Thus many talented young men would fail to continue preparation for the skills America so desperately needs. They could return to school only if there would be adequate government subsidy for their education and their families. Such subsidy is not likely to accompany a permanent conscription program such as has been proposed, both because of the expense and because it would be an inducement for boys to leave the army when the army wanted them to pursue a military career. Even if Congress should decide to subsidize in peacetime all the men who want to go to college after their period of universal military service, it would not be desirable to tie higher education to military service.

Moreover, many of those who did go to college and graduate school after doing their military service, would be further penalized since the army could expect to get doctors, engineers, scientists and technicians only from this group. Thus, the specialists upon whom the military place such great dependence would face a draft both before and after their university training. Such double service would be neither fair nor equitable.

There are other grave problems that would result from universal military service. Any program that was truly universal would also draft women. Some government and army officials have already suggested this. The dangers to the American home as well as to the nation are apparent from the dislocations during the war years. Juvenile delinquency resulting from mothers and older sisters being engaged in long hours of war work during the last war would be intensified a hundred-fold as young women were put in the army and older women replaced them in industry.

Similarly, if all young men, including those physically unfit for military service but otherwise able to work, were taken from farms and factories, our economy would be seriously injured.

A program of universal military service would also be an entering wedge for a labor draft such as the army demanded during the last war. News reports of official thinking about universal military service reveal that boys rejected as unfit for military service would be trained for civilian defense and other defense jobs and would presumably be expected to stay in these jobs at army pay while other boys remained in the army. Not only would this be a labor draft but such draftees would be employed at jobs normally performed by nonconscript labor. This would be involuntary servitude.

Since all who had universal military service would thereafter be in the reserves and subject to military call, no special legislation would be required if the government wanted to subject workers to "work or fight" orders, to prevent strikes, or in other ways to control the manpower of the nation—a further reason for regarding universal military service as a type of labor draft. . . .

One important reason for a lot of emotional thinking about universal military service needs to be examined. The idea that everyone owes an obligation to his country should not be perverted into the idea that everyone must fulfill his duty in the same way. A citizen's obligation to the community is a continuing one which is not fulfilled by submitting to the compulsion of the state for a few years. The compulsion of the state may actually interfere with or destroy a person's preparation to fulfill his obligation to his country or keep him from rendering his best service. America has risen to greatness not because of any authoritarian requirement that all fit into the same mold but because it fostered the basic spirit of voluntary community responsibility. The essence of democratic belief is that man was not made for the state, but that the state was created to serve its citizens. If our country were to pass a universal military training and service program it would jeopardize our democracy and mortgage our future with the European pattern of permanent conscription.

WE MUST AVOID PERMANENT MILITARIZATION [6]

Either military security demands universal military training or it does not. If it does demand it, then we should adopt it. If not, then we should not adopt it. It is on this basis that I shall attempt to present the case and the points against UMT.

1. The successful defense of our country under present conditions depends upon our readiness to meet an attack with overwhelming power, immediately available. Specifically, it means

---

[6] "Should We Have Universal Military Training?" by Alonzo F. Myers, chairman, Department of Education, New York University. *Parents' Magazine.* 26:27+. January 1951. Reprinted by permission.

that we must have ready for immediate duty powerful, well-trained, air, naval and mobile ground forces. UMT makes no contribution toward such a state of immediate readiness. In fact, the diversion of trained military personnel to UMT training duties would work against such a state.

As Hanson Baldwin pointed out in the New York *Times* (May 4, 1949): "Attack can come to the United States, and we can attack any enemy, only through the air or by sea. In the initial phase of any war of any nature using any weapons, what is of primary and fundamental importance is, therefore, control of the air and the sea. Emphasis, therefore, should be on insular strategy as opposed to continental strategy, on air-sea strategy as opposed to mass army strategy." That statement is just as true today as it was in 1949.

2. The great development of long-range bombers and of atomic weapons that has taken place in recent years has given a terrific advantage to the side that chooses to launch a surprise attack as a means of starting a war. We have reason to fear such an attack. Our country has no intention of becoming an aggressor nation. We shall not start a war. Our best defense against such an attack must lie in the threat of immediate, tremendous and overwhelming retaliation.

We cannot build any Maginot Line, whether consisting of UMT or anything else, that will protect us against any and all forms of attack. But we can establish and maintain a powerful, instantly ready, striking force consisting of planes, guided missiles, guided missile launchers, aircraft carriers, submarines and airborne troops which can be ready to strike at once against any enemy that attacks us. Of course, such a force will require manpower, but it must be skilled manpower, immediately ready manpower. UMT will not help with that.

3. It is argued that because Russia has 200 divisions, while we have only a small fraction of that number, we should adopt UMT. If the outcome of any conflict between our country and any conceivable combination of allies, and Russia and her probable allies, were to depend upon which side could place the largest number of foot soldiers in the field, we would be sure to lose the war. Yet it would be in pursuit of the impossible

task of trying to match Russia's manpower that we would adopt UMT.

It has been said by its proponents that we should adopt UMT in order to present a strong military posture, the idea being that this would impress Russia and discourage her from starting a war. It would impress Russia, all right, but it might make her think that we had lost our minds. Russia would not be impressed by whatever number of boys to whom we might give universal military training. She could always double or treble that number. Russia would know that if we were spending three to four billion dollars a year on UMT, we would be taking that amount from the development and maintenance of powerful military forces in existence.

4. Actually, UMT is an exceedingly costly and inefficient way by which to attempt to maintain a strong military establishment. At best, the training would be outmoded within two to three years after it had been received. Not only is that true, but it also is true that a great majority of the men to whom the training would be given would not be called for duty with the armed forces if war did come. A great majority would be kept at essential civilian tasks on the farms and in the factories, producing the necessary food and equipment for the prosecution of the war. UMT would not help them with those tasks.

5. It is quite true that we are still a long way from the time of the so-called "push-button" war, and that any war in which we may be engaged in the near future will require large numbers of men in the armed forces before it is successfully terminated. It is true that airpower alone is not likely to win a war. The time for the employment of large numbers of ground troops, however, is not in the beginning stages of a war. Without clear supremacy in the air and on the sea, we would never get to the point of being able to make use of large numbers of ground troops.

Our critical task is not that of procuring and training large numbers of military manpower. That task is relatively simple as compared with that of providing enough up-to-date equipment. Which means that it is our industrial potential and our research, development and production of military weapons that will determine our readiness for war if it comes, rather than the number of men who might be given universal military training. It has been true in the past, it was true in Korea, and it will be true in the future, that we can procure and train men faster than we can equip them.

6. We are the only really strong industrial nation in the world today, aside from Russia. We are making a desperate effort to arm our allies. Unless and until we arm them, they are helpless. For their protection they need our airpower, our unquestioned mastery of the seas and our arms. They do not need mass manpower from us. That is the one important asset that they have. UMT will not protect Western Europe from successful attack and devastation by Russia. It is our industrial might, incomparably stronger than Russia's, that will provide this protection.

7. The direct and the indirect cost of UMT would be so great that, in order to indulge ourselves in this costly luxury, we would almost surely starve the really essential elements in our national defense. We urgently need a greatly strengthened diplomatic service. We have never had, except in wartime, a first-rate intelligence service. Inadequate intelligence is almost as bad as no intelligence at all. We should, for example, have been better informed about the plans of the North Koreans than we were. Our "Voice of America" broadcasts and other means of communicating with the people behind the Iron Curtain need increased financial support. Our military research and development program must not be permitted to lag behind that of any possible future enemy. We still lack an adequate radar warning system. One of the greatest hazards connected with the adoption of UMT is that it would give us a false sense of security.

8. Finally, UMT and the further intensification of the armaments race which its adoption would entail are not and can never be the answer to our problem of security. In the next war, even the victor will not win. We shall not be secure until the threat of war is banished from the world.

The American people are ready and willing to take all measures essential to the defense of their country. But they draw a sharp distinction between the need of a draft when it is necessary to procure military manpower and the adoption of universal military training as a permanent policy for the United States. Peacetime conscription, except in times of grave emergency, is abhorrent to freedom-loving Americans and is essentially un-American. An increasing number of Americans are convinced that our ultimate security lies, not in the permanent militarization of our country, but in the strengthening of the United Nations and the development of an international police force that will be powerful enough to discourage aggression on the part of any member of the family of nations.

"TRIUMPH OF THE MELANCHOLY MEN" [7]

This country has sadly and soberly recognized the need for building up its military establishment to deter Soviet aggression. None of us knows the duration and scope of the emergency; we do know the draft can supply the manpower we need. [Universal military training] raises totally different issues. It is based on the proposition that we must decisively alter our traditional attitudes toward militarism. We dissent. The United States was able to meet the threat of fascism without resort to UMT. We do not need it to meet the Soviet challenge.

This nation has historically resisted proposals for a system of universal training on the good ground that it means the acceptance of militarization as a permanent aspect of our society. We do not happen to be terrified by the spectre of imminent military dictatorship; but we have a healthy respect for the view that a universal military training setup won't bring out the best in American life. At this juncture a large army is an unpleasant necessity. Nothing has happened, however, to prove that the army builds character or that we should look to generals for the guidance, stimulation and spiritual feeding of our young men.

The army has tried in every past emergency to sell UMT to the American people. The sale has never been made; there is no new justification for it. It is true that the draft requires improvisation. That is the nature of a free society's defense. But

[7] From "The Army's Big Offensive"—an editorial. New York *Post.* p26. April 3, 1951. Reproduced by permission from New York *Post.* Copyright 1951, New York Post Corp.

the spontaneous weapons of free men always emerge in time of crisis. They have never failed us.

The thing that concerns us most is the psychological impact of passage of a military training law. Our foreign policy is based on the premise that aggression can be finally averted if we build up the strength of the free world, create a true system of collective security through the United Nations, restore the economic health of Western Europe and give new aid and leadership to Asia's non-Communist millions. We have rejected the idea of "preventive" or "inevitable" war. We are saying there is still hope for peace and stability in our time if we are resolute and purposeful. The cracks that have appeared in the Soviet empire in recent months give further promise of better things to come. Why choose this moment to proclaim that the crisis can never end?

Universal military training is the triumph of the melancholy men. It is an announcement that we have abandoned hope of achieving any serenity in this century. It is a victory for those who say we must model our society on the totalitarianism system in order to save freedom.

We say again that no man can tell whether the world's tensions will be resolved in two years or twenty or whether the Soviet rulers will take the ultimate gamble of total war in the foreseeable future. We do know that a society which tells all its children that for all time to come they face UMT is a society in which the brass-hats have won an eminence we have never before accorded them, and reasonable men have admitted their failure. Once the military system is imposed the face of America will be altered. If the world ever achieves a happier time, let no man believe the Army will graciously yield the power it has won under UMT.

UNIVERSAL MILITARY SERVICE: A STERN PROGRAM FOR SURVIVAL [8]

Neither the present Selective Service Act nor proposals for universal military training seem to give promise of assuring a

[8] From an article by James Bryant Conant, president of Harvard University. *Look.* 14:33-5. December 19, 1950. Reprinted by permission.

continuing armed force of 3 to 3.5 million men. A training program provides only reserves; what is needed now is a force in being. What seems to be required is a universal military service of two years for all able-bodied youth before they take their places in the industrial life of the country.

I suggest that every young man on reaching the age of 18 or on graduation from high school be enrolled in the service of Uncle Sam for two years, with a firm moral commitment on the part of the government that, barring a global war, the service would be for only two years.

I say "every young man" advisedly: the able-bodied to serve in the armed forces; those physically unfit to serve in other capacities at the same pay, which should not be high.

There should be no deferments or exemptions for college students or anyone else. Indeed, the difficulties of attempting to defer from the draft any one type of student are already proving to be formidable; yet to interrupt professional training seems unwise. To defer military service until a young man's education is complete may mean deferring it four to eight years. It would be better for most individuals to get their tour of duty in uniform over and done with before they enter college.

If we are to have an armed force of over three million men, I see no practical alternative to the simple, clear-cut proposition of having absolutely no exemptions from the two years of service. The reasons are compelling to have this service performed before a young man begins his post-high-school education and before he takes his place in the productive activities of the nation. If such a proposal were to become the law of the land, the educational institutions would have to make drastic readjustments, admittedly. A great sacrifice in both the area of general or liberal education and in professional training would be the consequence. But I, for one, have with much reluctance come to the conclusion that such sacrifices are demanded by the extreme peril which the free world now faces.

It is hardly necessary to point out that legislation to accomplish the ends advocated in this article would supplement, not supplant, the present selective service law. Selective service is in essence a mechanism for raising an army with the minimum interference with the life of the country. It is based on the assumption that the men will be drawn from productive activities and that the local boards are best able to decide who can be drafted with the minimum disruption of the life of the community.

The proposed two-year universal military service for young men 18-20 years of age would require no local administration; it taps a pool of manpower before that manpower has to any considerable degree become involved in the productive activity of the nation. However, the maximum number of able-bodied men thus available is only about two million (a million per age group). Therefore, recruiting would have to continue at a vigorous pace; likewise, selective service would have to be kept in reserve, for use in event of a global war and possibly to supplement the universal service of the 19-20-year group. For the next year or two, a combination of selective service for the age group 20-25, and the proposed universal service would be required for the degree of mobilization here envisioned.

The problem of supplying officers for the increased armed forces can be met for the next few years by calling on the reserve corps, on the one hand, and by the training of officer material in the present college population on the other. By suitable arrangements under selective service, a supply of medical officers can be assured for the next five to seven years by recruiting from men now enrolled in colleges or universities. But if a universal service law is enacted, a problem will eventually arise as to the selection of line officers and specialists from the age groups subject to this law. There are difficulties here, admittedly, but they are by no means insuperable.

If educational benefits are provided for those who have served two years in uniform (as they might well be), these benefits could be in part related to the student's willingness to serve later as an officer. But to discuss these matters or to consider how professional training could best be shortened to compensate for the time lost in service would be to divert attention from the main issue: Is the United States willing to make the effort necessary to meet the challenge of the times? If so, what alternative is there to mobilizing the youth of the nation by a two-year call to arms?

In conclusion, I should like to emphasize both the urgency of increasing our armed forces with the aim of defending Europe and the long-range nature of the undertaking. As an emergency measure, National Guard units and reserves can be ordered into active service. But these sources of older manpower are clearly unsuitable for a large standing army for a period of years. The continuous replenishment of the armed forces on a long-term planning basis seems required. The advantages of building up over the years a reserve pool of men with two years of service who could be mobilized for a global war are so obvious that no comment is required.

UNIVERSAL MILITARY SERVICE: TOTAL CONSCRIPTION WILL HURT AMERICA [9]

Universal military service was long tried in countries like Germany, Austria, Italy, France and Russia. There is little evidence that it produced the good by-products often claimed for it—an improvement in democracy, patriotism or national health. It is, therefore, to be judged from a military point of view. But it is an odd fact that the only major powers victorious in both world wars (Great Britain, the United States) were the only ones that did not have UMS. Though their victory had many other causes, it came in part because they were able flexibly to create armed forces designed to meet the needs of the war then going on. They did not have to use a military machine made to meet the conditions encountered in a previous war. One of the virtues of Dr. Conant's plan [10] is its apparent simplicity. One of its weaknesses is its inflexibility. But it is also true that in the next war we may not have time to create a new army.

The kind of military strength we need now is certainly changing. From 1793 to 1918 was the period of the supremacy of massed manpower. But World War II saw an increasing importance for the machine and the specialist—the tank driver, the

[9] From an article by Charles Woolsey Cole, president of Amherst College. *Look.* 15:54-5. January 2, 1951. Reprinted by permission.
[10] See "A Stern Program for Survival," above.

jet pilot, the radar operator. Today, moreover, the scientist, the engineer, the surgeon and the production expert behind the lines are vital parts of our military power.

We cannot compete with Russia (much less Russia plus satellites plus China) in raw manpower. Where we can compete is in trained, educated, skilled manpower. Because we educate a larger proportion of our youth than any other country, we can provide our armed forces with more specialists and back up our armed forces with more specialists than any other country. But this source of strength is ours only so long as we continue to train young men. Dr. Conant's proposal, any way you implement it, will cause a two-year gap in our flow of trained youth, a gap that will never be made up, a break in our lifeline in the most crucial decade of our history.

Even if we provide GI-type benefits (at a cost of untold billions) for those who have served under UMS, many able boys will not, at 20, go to college and on to professional schools. They will take jobs and get married. Thus, we will not only make a two-year gap in the flow, we will thin it down once it is renewed.

We should not take every fit boy as he comes from high school and put him untrained and unskilled into uniform. Rather, we should save out some of the ablest (say 60,000 to 80,000 a year) and see to it that they go to college, and in many cases to graduate school, so that they may better serve the armed forces and the nation with the added skills and knowledge they will have acquired.

There is even something unconvincing about Dr. Conant's figures. He proposes to create armed forces of 3 to 3.5 million men largely by two-year UMS. Only about 1.05 million boys reach 18 annually. Of these, only about 750,000 are fit for military duties. But .75 plus .75 equals only 1.5. So, unless we raise the term of service to three or four years, we will have to find outside of UMS another 1.5 to 2 million, by voluntary enlistment, draft, or the extensive use of women for noncombat service. If we can find that many, we can find another 75,000 each year to replace those whose education is being continued.

There is another difficulty with this UMS plan. Even if we supply the Defense Department with 1.5 million untrained 18 and 19 year olds, the armed forces will still need specialists of all sorts—scientists, engineers, doctors, dentists, economists, accountants. In a few years, those educated before UMS will become unavailable and we will have to turn to those who have done UMS. This will mean double service for a great many technicians and specialists. . . .

Another kind of objection to Dr. Conant's plan comes from the fact that, under it, 18 and 19 year olds would be used for fighting, garrison and occupation duties. In fighting, the record shows that the performance of such boys is excellent. But at posts in foreign countries and in occupied lands, they might not be mature enough or stable enough to resist temptations thrust at them. Their morale might easily be impaired.

Two further objections are worth a glance. First, the Defense Department plans to rely heavily on ROTC for officer training. UMS might well destroy the ROTC. It might be hard to get 20 year olds just out from two years' service to enlist in the ROTC and obligate themselves for two years' more service. Second, the transition from the present Selective Service System to UMS, or the retention of two different systems of recruitment, might be very clumsy to manage. It might raise most serious problems just at a time when we need to be strong and alert.

There are economic as well as military difficulties under Dr. Conant's plan. One is the cost of providing GI-type benefits for those who have done UMS. Yet without such aid, enough young men may not go to college. Another is the staggering expense of feeding, clothing, and training the physically and mentally unfit. It might well run to two billions a year. (Just to keep our perspective, let us remember that all the buildings of all the colleges and universities in the country have been valued at five billions). Then, too, the shock to our economy would be serious if we swept into service from farms and factories all 18 and 19 year olds. Many 4Fs can do such jobs. Leaving them at work would cushion the shock somewhat.

From an educational point of view, Dr. Conant's type of UMS is a leap in the dark. We cannot know how it would affect our society. In this respect, the experience of other countries that have had UMS will not help us, for all of them have granted educational deferments, and none has drafted the unfit. We do not know, despite our experiences with GIs, whether 20-26 is as good an age for learning as 18-24. We cannot guess how many able men will turn aside from further education, after a two-year break. We cannot guess the long-run effects of giving every American male into the hands of the military for two of his most formative years.

We can be sure, however, that the five lean years Dr. Conant's proposal would impose on higher education (three years with 50 per cent or less of normal male enrollment, two years with 75 per cent or less) would necessitate costly federal aid to our colleges and universities and might bring them to some degree under government control.

There are other more subtle problems. There is, for example, an unusual fact of which Dr. Conant is well aware. Almost all great scientific discoveries, basic new ideas, from those of Newton to Einstein, have been developed by very young men, usually men under 30, often under 25. Youth seems necessary for the daring leaps of scientific imagination. Today, science is so complex that it takes five or ten years after high school to get out to the scientific frontiers where advances can be made. To add two years to the time required to get to the point where such contributions are possible might slow our scientific progress. . . .

One can agree with Dr. Conant this far: In the present state of the world, we must maintain very large armed forces. Therefore, every fit young man will probably have to serve the nation, sooner or later, for a period of something like two years. But the question of when and how that service should be rendered still remains. There are, perhaps, other and better solutions than Dr. Conant's.

UNIVERSAL MILITARY SERVICE IN BRITAIN [11]

The National Service Act, 1947 (which became law on July 18, 1947), provided that from January 1, 1949, until January 1,

[11] From a study by the British Information Services, Reference Division (ID 1041). New York. 1951. p2-5. Reprinted by permission.

1954, all male British subjects who had reached the age of 18 and had not reached the age of 26, and who had not served in the armed forces before January 1, 1947, would be liable for compulsory military service. "National Servicemen," as they were to be called, would serve for twelve months whole time in the regular forces, and six years part time in the reserve, a total of seven years in all. During the period of part-time service, they were obliged to do not more than 60 days' training, of which not more than 21 days could be served in any one year. . . .

The National Service Act, 1948, consolidated the previous acts to 1947 and the Reinstatement in Civil Employment Act, 1944. The National Service (amendment) Act, 1948, increased the term of whole-time service from 12 months to 18 months, and reduced the aggregate of whole-time and part-time service from seven years to five and a half years. . . .

Recruiting for the armed forces continued to be inadequate, and in August 1950, after the outbreak of war in Korea, the term of whole-time service for National Servicemen was extended to two years, the term of part-time service being correspondingly reduced to three and a half years. This became effective on October 1, 1950, under the National Service Act, 1950.

The National Service Acts did not apply to women, nor to Northern Ireland, where service with the armed forces continued on a voluntary basis.

Between June 1945 and August 1950, about a million young men underwent compulsory military training. At the time of registration, a man could express a preference for a particular branch of service, i.e. the Royal Navy, the Army, or the Royal Air Force, but no guarantee could be given that a National Serviceman would be posted according to his preference. The majority of men continued to serve in the army. . . .

After training, a National Serviceman was required to do part-time service in the territorial army or one of the reserve or auxiliary forces. Part-time service normally took effect on the day following that on which whole-time service was completed. . . . National Servicemen were generally required to take steps to enlist in the territorial army or appropriate reserve sometime prior to the completion of their whole-time service. As with whole-time service, men were allowed to express a preference for a particular reserve force or unit within that force, and again every effort was made to post National Servicemen according to their preferences, although this could not always be done. . . .

The only persons who were not liable to be called up for military training under the National Service Acts, 1948, were men in government service outside Great Britain, men in holy orders or ministers of any religious denomination, and insane and blind persons.

Deferment of call-up was not granted on industrial grounds except to men employed in the basic industries of coal mining or agriculture. By special arrangement in 1949, a limited number of deferments was granted to cotton operatives. Men employed in the merchant navy were deferred in 1949 owing to the limited number of vacancies for National Servicemen in the Royal Navy. Men who were in reserved occupations during World War II, and were under 26 years of age, were liable for call-up under the National Service Acts, 1948.

Apprentices, learners, and students could make special request for deferment if they were able to satisfy the authorities that they were undergoing essential training. (For apprentices, it was necessary to furnish proof of a bona fide apprenticeship.) Deferment was also granted to young men in order to sit for school-leaving or university-qualifying examinations. At the same time, it was possible for young men planning to proceed to universities after training to request permission to enter upon their military training at any time between 17 years and 2 months and $17\frac{1}{2}$ years, if this would aid in any training or career they intended to take up later.

Doctors and dentists were liable for call-up at any time up to the age of 30 years. . . .

The National Service Act, 1947, had a generally favorable reception in Britain, and was supported in the main by the two major political parties. At the Labor Party Conference at Margate on May 26, 1947, the resolution supporting the government's conscription policy was passed by a vote of 2,332,000 to 571,000, and while several speakers emphasized their dislike of having to adopt such a measure, they agreed with the need for it.

UNIVERSAL CONSCRIPTION 97

There was some criticism of, but no opposition to, the extension of whole-time service from 18 months to two years. Assurance was given by the Secretary of State for War, Mr. [John] Strachey, during the Debate on National Service in the House of Commons, September 15, 1950, that it was not the government's intention to make conscription a permanent feature of the armed services. He pointed out that, under the National Service Acts, 1948, no man could be liable for call-up after December 31, 1953, and that, should the international situation and the flow of volunteers into the regular forces permit, the period of whole-time service could and would be reviewed, and, if possible, decreased.

CONSCRIPTION FOR ESSENTIAL SERVICE

EDITOR'S INTRODUCTION

This section deals with the heart of the problem raised in this volume: Should the government have the power to draft all adults for essential service in time of war?

The United States Government has never considered, in concrete terms, such a sweeping proposition. The closest this nation ever approached it was during World War II, when Congress debated a national service act which would apply to all men, and to women between the ages of 18 and 50.

The 78th Congress (1943-44) debated this measure, which was sponsored by Representative James W. Wadsworth (Republican of New York) and Senator Warren R. Austin (Republican of Vermont). This bill did not get beyond the stage of committee discussion.

With the renewed urging of President Franklin D. Roosevelt, another national service measure was introduced in the 79th Congress in 1945. The House passed the bill, 246-165. It would have enabled local draft boards to order males between the ages of 18 and 45 to remain in essential positions or to move into such jobs from other employment. The Senate rejected this bill, substituting a milder one of its own. The Senate bill would have empowered the War Manpower Commission chairman to fix employment ceilings and to prohibit or regulate hiring of new workers in all industries. The measure was approved by the Senate, 63-16.

A compromise of the two bills was worked out to give the Director of War Mobilization authority to "freeze" workers in their jobs, fix employment ceilings, and regulate or prohibit hiring. The measure would apply to all civilians. This version was approved by the House, 167-160, but the Senate, on April 3, 1945, rejected it, 29-46. With the end of hostilities in Europe the following month, further discussion of a national service act ceased.

While much of the material in this section is drawn from the World War II period, the basic arguments remain valid for today. Wartime experiences in another democratic country Britain) and in one of the enemy totalitarian nations (Japan) are also included.

OVERVIEW OF COMPULSORY NATIONAL SERVICE [1]

Civilian manpower authority in some degree is in general accepted in time of war. However, the specific kind and degree of manpower controls to be employed are not an equally foregone conclusion. Present schools of thought about manpower controls for a future war split in two main groups: (*a*) those favoring the compulsions and penalties approach of a national service act from the start; and (*b*) those favoring controls that maximize the voluntary drives of the individual, but channel them in an orderly, guided pattern. Both approaches claim for their methods more success in achieving what is the common goal of each—namely, the greatest production results.

Perhaps the choice between them might in the actual event of all-out war depend upon the temper of labor and the public. In the case of a degree of national danger greater than any heretofore experienced, more direct and sweeping manpower controls might prove necessary and therefore acceptable. . . .

Broadly speaking, national service where exercised has involved governmental authority to assign both workers and employers to given tasks; to hold them to those tasks, or to reassign them at will; to recruit new workers and new employers; to prohibit their efforts in nonessential production; and to maximize their efforts on behalf of essential production. In this country, national service as debated in the wartime Wadsworth bill was more restricted to measures necessary to utilize manpower effectively. In those instances in which the principle has been applied—as in the case of Britain and Germany in World

---

[1] From *Mobilization Planning and the National Security* (1950-60), by William Y. Elliott, consultant in industrial mobilization of the Legislative Reference Service, Library of Congress. Senate Document No. 204, 81st Congress, 2d session. Superintendent of Documents. Washington, D.C. 1950. p80-5.

War II—it has been accompanied by governmental authority over community facilities in order to free workers and employers as much as possible for the demands of greater production.

The British achieved the system of compulsions and penalties involved in national service in almost a single sentence, to wit—that each individual owes his person and his property to the service of His Majesty (the Crown as the symbol of national unity and ideals) in time of war.[2]

Arguments in favor of national service (wartime draft of civilian labor). The case for a national service act at the start of a war effort is the case of necessity that production must come first if survival is at stake. The rationale is the rationale of the democratic procedure. Thus, it is argued, that since the government arbitrarily assigns manpower to the military pool in the first instance, and then arbitrarily assigns manpower within the military pool in the second instance, that it is only fair that the principle of equality of sacrifice should be borne also by the residual civilian pool. The gap between men in uniform and those out of uniform is alleged to have always been bad for morale. The soldier resents the freedom and the higher wages of the civilian, and the civilian feels guilty about his security and comfort. "The duty to work and the duty to fight would make soldier and worker equals."

The new weapons potentials make it unrealistic to assume the easy, manageable conditions of World War II, where in retrospect there was plenty of time as well as plenty of manpower, compared with the probabilities that would face the country in the event of another world engagement. This time controls must be prompt; they must be complete; they must be integrated with production and stabilization controls from the beginning. As a nation we are the last to be content to rest our security on outmoded administrative procedures. In short, to hold on uncompromisingly to a question of rights just on principle, may result in the loss of those rights permanently.

Again the government is alleged to be in the best position to balance the interests of the worker and the employer jointly against the interests of the nation as a whole, certainly in time of war, though not necessarily in time of peace. It is argued

[2] See selection below on British manpower controls in World War II.—Ed.

that the legal rights of both will be better protected than either alone when left to the comparative bargaining fortuities of each in free competition.

Even the very discussion of such authority is said to be salutary as an inducement to exhaust in debate all other proposed controls while there is still time to spend on debate. But it should always be remembered that if there is no such direct legal power on the books in stand-by form, devious methods of indirect control will have to be contrived by the government in an emergency which will never be really adequate.

The perfect example that such drastic controls can work in a wartime democracy without affecting the democratic attitude of mind is to be found in Britain's successful experience with a national service act in World War II.

A national service scheme need not direct every individual to each job. There is no reason it should not take a form like that of Britain's act, directing manpower to certain essential occupation types of industrial production, farming, transportation, etc., rather than to specific jobs. This would carry further the experience of the last war, and would, if coupled with compulsory legal powers, draft exemptions, and incentives, be a more manageable administrative scheme, it is argued, than individual selective service mobilization of all workers. But the border line cases of civilian essentiality present grave difficulties in any case.

Arguments against a national service act. Those who oppose the idea of a national service act claim that it is undemocratic and probably unconstitutional for the United States; that it will inhibit production rather than enhance it; that it is an oversimplification of the job to be done; that administratively it is not feasible; and that it is unnecessary because there are better alternatives that touch the mainspring of American effort in voluntary cooperation. . . .

It is argued that in a national service act the fundamental legal rights of an individual are jeopardized—for example, in such things as the right to work where, when, and for whom one pleases, and the equivalent right of the employer to hire whom he pleases. There are said to be very material differences between conscripting for the armed services, and conscripting for the benefit and profit of another individual—in this case, a private employer. A situation where an employer makes money on the forced labor of an employee approximates slave labor which is prohibited by the Constitution.

Regardless of how one might argue that a national service act would control both employer and worker, the fact of the matter is that the real bite would be on the worker. The businessman can produce one item as well as another as long as his earnings are vouchsafed and his financial losses covered as they would be, but it may be a personal hardship of the most acute nature for a worker to have to stay on a job for which he considers himself unfit and in psychological conflict. Even if the employer must cease producing something unessential and has to go out of business, the worker loses his livelihood along with the producer's loss of business, and his particular training may not again be utilized. So the employer loses an investment in money, but the worker loses an investment in skill and experience—a much more personal kind of loss. But [for the most part] . . . war production is more profitable than peacetime production, if only because the output will be at peak volume. The employer reaps profits from what he is compelled to produce, but the worker will in all probability not share commensurately in the increased profits. Nor can the worker even receive the postwar emoluments given to the soldier, such as pensions, bonuses, hospital privileges, attractive insurance, and job preferences.

Moreover, if it is increased worker productivity that is desired, that occurs under free choice, not under compulsion. Indeed, inefficient as democracies are alleged to be, they have in the end been more efficient than dictatorships in war because their economic output, resting on voluntary cooperation and the competitive drive, has always yielded a greater productivity than the labor of a dictatorship. Indeed, compulsory service, while it might assure the direction of production in given categories, would inhibit it in the end. Proof of this is to be found in the experience of national socialism in Germany where productivity declined despite controls, compulsions, and fears. In short, just merely moving people around or preventing them from moving around does not make them produce. What is really wanted is their production, not the authority to try to make them produce.

To be sure, if the government plans to take over all industry and run it, then labor has fewer grounds for complaint about discrimination than if only the worker were compelled to take a job and stay with it. But who would advocate that drastic an approach to production? One has only to remember the experience of the government in running the railroads, the telegraph and telephone facilities, to realize that the cure is worse than the disease. Moveover, "the right of a worker to quit and the corresponding right of an employer to discharge, constitute primary factors in the shaping of their employment relationship. Nevertheless, deprivation of the right to quit and the right to discharge in effect leaves the relationship without a rudder." But, assuming that the government would have to control materials and facilities—thereby indirectly controlling the employer and the employee—and even granting that it might do a good job, it would not have to worry about protecting these inorganic things the way it would really have to worry about protecting labor. That job in itself would consume more manpower than it would conserve by the compulsion technique. Not only would the government have to assign jobs, but it would have to supervise hours, wages, working conditions.

At the peak of World War II there were over 12 million men in the armed services. Their skills were never used to the full because administratively it was impossible to match their individual skills against appropriate niches. Suppose that the administrative job should be increased to the proportions of having to find appropriate niches for 50 to 60 millions. How utterly impossible it would be to handle. There would never be enough men skilled enough in the one job of placement, to say nothing of the magnitude of the training job that would ensue. And the record-keeping involved in handling even a portion of a 50 to 60 million persons operation staggers the imagination and the public purse—just in the comparative terms of the record job undertaken by the Veterans' Administration on one tenth the number. No, . . . it is a gross oversimplification to assume that all the government has to do is to assign a man to a niche and that's an end to the problem. On the contrary, it would be the beginning of a series of problems. Furthermore, how much simpler it is for the government to control employers who are much fewer in numbers than to try to control the mass of the workers. The latter get controlled indirectly in any event, but in a much easier, more painless way.

And after all, what is the point of compulsory service in the last analysis? Most people not only have to work for a living, but they want to work, and especially under the stimulus of a patriotic motive. Only a few congenital idlers are recalcitrant. And if it is to garner those few into the ranks, it would scarcely be worth the effort and expense because they would probably not be good producers anyway. This is the heavy artillery approach to the blue-jay game—highly inappropriate.

Even assuming that the administrative burden is not altogether impossible—such is the view of those who say that there is a tendency to exaggerate the administrative burden—on substantive grounds, if not on procedural, the case against national service is argued as incontrovertible. Every time the government makes an individual assignment, it must follow through with a long series of safeguards. It has to be sure that the job is not substandard as to health and safety; that there are housing facilities available; that previous seniority and pension rights are not sacrificed; that workmen's compensation is available; that there are medical facilities within reach; that the hours of work are not too long; and other similar safeguards. It is at this point that both the substantive and the procedural problems get out of hand.

Moreover, if the situation is serious enough for the government to have to put direct controls on labor as well as on employers, it would have to do many things that would be far more serious—such as commandeering private housing, establishing communal nurseries, feeding destitute peoples and the like. Under these circumstances compulsory labor control would be accepted without much question. But short of such disaster conditions, it does not make sense in the light of other available alternatives that capitalize on the voluntary cooperation motive, such as:

(*a*) Employment ceilings that tell employers and workers alike that they may employ so many men, but not exactly which ones;

(*b*) Labor priorities which indicate the needs for manpower without determining specifically who should go where;

(c) Displacement of workers and employers in nonessential production which is still an impersonal approach leaving plenty of latitude for voluntary choices in reemployment;

(d) Public employment offices in shortage areas which make it possible to refer kinds of skill, as distinct from particular persons, to and from congested areas;

(e) Job simplification, discharge, and upgrading as placement techniques which give the employer and the employee wide latitude in personal choice.

In brief, the alternatives stimulate both employer and employee to work out their own problems on a mutually agreeable basis, rather than to have to live with them on a mutually disagreeable basis.

Current status of proposals for manpower controls in the event of war. There is no official government position on the form that manpower controls would take in the event of another emergency. There are, of course, studies on all conceivable controls in this, as in other areas of mobilization planning. There is a consensus on the part of the civilian agencies against the application of a national service act, and there is a predisposition on the part of the military agencies in favor of such an act. Because of the predominant legal position of the civilian authorities, presumptively the national service approach would not be sanctioned short of the direst kind of disaster. To the extent that such a disaster did occur, it seems unlikely that the "safeguards" mentioned above would be able to be applied along with individual or group assignment. However, if a long pull on the labor supply ultimately required governmental "assignment" powers, the "national attitude" against conscription would probably compel a system of safeguards, and perhaps even inducements and rewards, as an accompaniment to any system of compulsions and penalties. Moreover, family housing and community facilities probably could not be ignored as areas for government concession. In any event, any system of manpower controls which would maintain civilian morale as well as war production requirements; which would minimize administrative burdens on the government; and which would not jeopardize economic stabilization through its financial cost; would seem to offer a sounder approach to manpower controls than one which rested solely on the basis of compulsions and penalties, yielding impersonal statistics of production output.

FDR'S PROPOSAL FOR NATIONAL SERVICE, I [3]

If ever there was a time to subordinate individual or group selfishness to the national good, that time is now. Disunity at home—bickerings, self-seeking, partisanship, stoppages of work, inflation, business as usual, politics as usual, luxury as usual—these are the influences which can undermine the morale of the brave men ready to die at the front for us here.

Those who are doing most of the complaining are not deliberately striving to sabotage the national war effort. They are laboring under the delusion that the time is past when we must make prodigious sacrifices—that the war is already won and we can begin to slacken off. But the dangerous folly of that point of view can be measured by the distance that separates our troops from their ultimate objectives in Berlin and Tokyo—and by the sum of all the perils that lie along the way.

Overconfidence and complacency are among our deadliest enemies. Last spring—after notable victories at Stalingrad and in Tunisia and against U-boats on the high seas—overconfidence became so pronounced that war production fell off. In two months, June and July, 1943, more than a thousand airplanes that could have been made and should have been made were not made. Those who failed to make them were not on strike. They were merely saying, "The war's in the bag—so let's relax!"

That attitude on the part of anyone—government or management or labor—can lengthen this war. It can kill American boys.

Let us remember the lessons of 1918. In the summer of that year the tide turned in favor of the Allies. But this government did not relax. In fact, our national effort was stepped up. In August 1918, the draft age limits were broadened from 21-31 to 18-45. The President called for "force to the utmost," and his call was heeded. And in November, only three months later, Germany surrendered.

[3] From President Franklin D. Roosevelt's annual message to Congress, January 11, 1944. *Current History.* 6:243-9. March 1944. Reprinted by permission.

That is the way to fight and win a war—all out—and not with half an eye on the battlefronts abroad and the other eye and a half on personal, selfish, or political interests here at home.

Therefore, in order to concentrate all our energies and resources on winning the war, and to maintain a fair and stable economy at home, I recommend that the Congress adopt:

1. A realistic tax law—which will tax all unreasonable profits, both individual and corporate, and reduce the ultimate cost of the war to our sons and daughters. . . .

2. A continuation of the law for the renegotiation of war contracts—which will prevent exorbitant profits and assure fair prices to the government. . . .

3. A cost of food law—which will enable the government (a) to place a reasonable floor under the prices the farmer may expect for his production, and (b) to place a ceiling on the prices a consumer will have to pay for the food he buys. . . .

4. Early enactment of the stabilization statute of October 1942. This expires June 30, 1944, and if it is not extended well in advance the country might just as well expect price chaos by summer. . . .

5. A national service law—which, for the duration of the war, will prevent strikes, and, with certain appropriate exceptions, will make available for war production or for any other essential services every able-bodied adult in the nation.

These five measures together form a just and equitable whole. I would not recommend a national service law unless the other laws were passed to keep down the cost of living, to share equitably the burdens of taxation, to hold the stabilization line, and to prevent undue profits.

The Federal Government already has the basic power to draft capital and property of all kinds for war purposes on a basis of just compensation.

As you know, I have for three years hesitated to recommend a national service act. Today, however, I am convinced of its necessity. Although I believe that we and our allies can win the war without such a measure, I am certain that nothing less than total mobilization of all our resources of manpower and capital will guarantee an earlier victory, and reduce the toll of suffering and sorrow and blood.

I have received a joint recommendation for this law from the heads of the War Department, the Navy Department and the Maritime Commission. These are the men who bear responsibility for the procurement of the necessary arms and equipment, and for the successful prosecution of the war in the field. They say:

When the very life of the nation is in peril the responsibility for service is common to all men and women. In such a time there can be no discrimination between the men and women who are assigned by the government to its defense at the battlefront and the men and women assigned to produce the vital materials essential to successful military operations. A prompt enactment of a national service law would be merely an expression of the universality of this responsibility.

I believe the country will agree that those statements are the solemn truth.

National service is the most democratic way to wage a war. Like selective service for the armed forces, it rests on the obligation of each citizen to serve his nation to his utmost where he is best qualified.

It does not mean reduction in wages. It does not mean loss of retirement. It does not mean that any substantial numbers of war workers will be disturbed in their present jobs. Let these facts be wholly clear.

Experience in other democratic nations at war—Britain, Canada, Australia, and New Zealand—has shown that the very existence of national service makes unnecessary the widespread use of compulsory power. National service has proved to be a unifying moral force—based on an equal and comprehensive legal obligation of all people in a nation at war.

There are millions of American men and women who are not in this war at all. It is not because they do not want to be in it. But they want to know where they can best do their share. National service provides that direction. It will be a means by which every man and woman can find that inner satisfaction which comes from making the fullest contribution to victory.

I know that all civilian workers will be glad to be able to say many years hence to their grandchildren: "Yes, I, too, was in service in the great war. I was on duty in an airplane factory, and I helped make hundreds of fighting planes. The government told me that in doing that I was performing my most useful work in the service of my country."

It is argued that we have passed the stage in the war where national service is necessary. But our soldiers and sailors know that that is not true. We are going forward on a long, rough road—and, in all journeys, the last miles are the hardest. And it is for that final effort—for the total defeat of our enemies—that we must mobilize our total resources. . . .

It is my conviction that the American people will welcome this win-the-war measure which is based on the eternally just principle of "Fair for one, fair for all."

It will give our people at home the assurance that they are standing four-square behind our soldiers and sailors. And it will give our enemies demoralizing assurance that we mean business—that we, 130 million Americans, are on the march to Rome, Berlin and Tokyo.

FDR'S PROPOSAL FOR NATIONAL SERVICE, II [4]

There are three basic arguments for a national service law. First, it would assure that we have the right numbers of workers in the right places at the right times. Second, it would provide supreme proof to all our fighting men that we are giving them what they are entitled to, which is nothing less than our total effort. And, third, it would be the final unequivocal answer to the hopes of the Nazis and the Japanese that we may become half-hearted about this war and that they can get from us a negotiated peace.

National service legislation would make it possible to put ourselves in a position to assure certain and speedy action in meeting our manpower needs. It would be used only to the extent absolutely required by military necessities. In fact, experience in Great Britain and in other nations at war indicates that use of the compulsory powers of national service is necessary only in rare instances. This proposed legislation would provide

[4] From President Franklin D. Roosevelt's annual message to Congress, January 6, 1945. *Vital Speeches of the Day.* 11:194-201. January 15, 1945. Reprinted by permission.

against loss of retirement and seniority rights and benefits. It would not mean reduction in wages.

In adopting such legislation, it is not necessary to discard the voluntary and cooperative processes which have prevailed up to this time. This cooperation has already produced great results. The contribution of our workers to the war effort has been beyond measure. We must build on the foundations that have already been laid and supplement the measures now in operation, in order to guarantee the production that may be necessary in the critical period that lies ahead.

At the present time we are using the inadequate tools at hand to do the best we can by such expedients as manpower ceilings, and the use of priority and other powers, to induce men and women to shift from nonessential to essential war jobs.

I am in receipt of a joint letter from the Secretary of War and the Secretary of the Navy, dated January 3, 1945, which says:

> With the experience of three years of war and after the most thorough consideration, we are convinced that it is now necessary to carry out the statement made by the Congress in the joint resolutions declaring that a state of war existed with Japan and Germany: That "to bring the conflict to a successful conclusion, all of the resources of the country are hereby pledged by the Congress of the United States."
>
> In our considered judgment . . . this requires total mobilization of our manpower by the passage of a war service law. The armed forces need this legislation to hasten the day of final victory, and to keep to a minimum the cost in lives.
>
> National war service, the recognition by law of the duty of every citizen to do his or her part in winning the war, will give complete assurance that the need for war equipment will be filled. In the coming year we must increase the output of many weapons and supplies on short notice. Otherwise we shall not keep our production abreast of the swiftly changing needs of war. At the same time it will be necessary to draw progressively many men now engaged in war production to serve with the armed forces, and their places in war production must be filled promptly. These developments will require the addition of hundreds of thousands to those already working in war industry. We do not believe that these needs can be met effectively under the present methods.
>
> The record made by management and labor in war industry has been a notable testimony to the resourcefulness and power of America. The needs are so great, nevertheless, that in many instances we have

been forced to recall soldiers and sailors from military duty to do work of a civilian character in war production, because of the urgency of the need for equipment and because of inability to recruit civilian labor.

WE MUST SUSPEND MANY RIGHTS AND PRIVILEGES [5]

We have proceeded a certain distance along toward mobilization [thus far in World War II]. To a very large degree we have mobilized industry. The Congress of the United States has placed it within the power of the Federal Government by statutes duly enacted to take over any industrial plant in America and operate it in the war effort. The government, in accordance with laws passed by the Congress, may step up to any employer or owner of a plant and say, "You must proceed to make a certain type of supply." That owner must do it lest the government take over the management and operation of the plant.

By laws enacted by the Congress, every contract made by an employer who is furnishing supplies to the government may be and is renegotiated, with the government the complete master of the final decision.

In accordance with an act of the Congress, the wages and salaries of every person employed in a plant from top to bottom may be and are fixed by executive order based upon law. Our tax laws, also enacted by the Congress, are devised, and I think correctly, to reduce profits to a minimum. The excess profits taxes on corporate incomes run as high as 90 per cent and correspondingly high on individual incomes. In other words, by the laws of the land, industry has been mobilized. We have not yet, however, by the process of any law whatsoever mobilized manpower. . . .

In some of the steps taken in the last two or three months in the direction of mobilizing manpower . . . the element of compulsion is present. I refer, for example, to the Work or Fight Order, directed to men between 18 and 38 years of age,

---

[5] From an address by James W. Wadsworth, Jr., former Republican member of the House of Representatives from New York, delivered before the Chamber of Commerce of the United States, April 27, 1943. *Vital Speeches of the Day.* 9:508-10. June 1, 1943. Reprinted by permission. As the date of this address indicates, Representative Wadsworth was one of the earliest Congressional proponents of a national service act during World War II.—Ed.

registered in the draft, with the clear intimation that if those men did not immediately or by April 1—and they are given leeway until May 1—find jobs in essential industry, they may be reclassified under the draft and put into the army or the navy. That is the threat. There is your element of compulsion. I think I can say to you that when the Congress passed the Selective Service Law it never expected or intended that that law should be used as a club to drive a citizen from one place to another.

And the recent order, well intended—I am not criticizing the intention of these steps—to the effect that no man may leave his job in an essential industry to take another job at a higher pay lest he be subjected to fine or imprisonment or both, cannot be found in any statute of the United States. It rests presumably upon the Stabilization Act of October 1942, but in that act the Congress authorized the government to freeze prices of commodities, salaries and wages—not men, they are not mentioned.

So I think it well to dispel the idea that we are proceeding solely in the voluntary spirit. I can mention some other orders because the element of compulsion, the implied threat, the indirect pressure, is back of nearly all of them.

We are the only great nation engaged in this war that is not completely mobilized . . . as to industry and manpower. Great Britain is completely mobilized, so is Australia, so is New Zealand, and, heaven knows, they are liberty-loving countries just as we are. Russia is completely mobilized. Every man and woman in Canada above the age of 16 is registered, and of course it goes without saying that our enemies are also completely mobilized. We alone stand halfway along this road. . . .

You have heard, of course, of the great pool of workers engaged in nonessential industries, men and women, upon which we must draw if we are to meet the demands of 1943-1944. The trouble is . . . that thousands and thousands of men and women anxious to work, anxious to help their country, don't know where to go or how to get there, and if they do find their way to the place, they don't know where they are going to live. There is no law on the subject whatsoever. The War Manpower Commission cannot today, for example, pay the traveling expenses of a person who moves from one community to another to take a war job. The War Manpower Commission has no power under the law today to see to it that proper housing awaits that person. The War Manpower Commission has no power, direct or implied, in the existing statutes, to assure that person that when the emergency is over he may return to his former employment and recover it. Not a word in any law we have! And unless my investigations are completely wrong, I find that the great deterrent standing in the way today of the recruiting of war workers from the nonessential industries is that atmosphere of complete uncertainty. They don't know.

More than that, many of them will tell you, as they have told me, "Yes, I am willing to go, leaving my nonessential job, into an essential job, if everybody else like me is treated the same way." There is no equality of obligation suggested by law to the people of the United States, none whatsoever.

It is a little disturbing to look ahead and measure this thing, if we can do so. It was not a pleasant thing to have Admiral [Emory S.] Land [U. S. Maritime Commission Chairman] come before the Military Affairs Committee of the House the other day and state that in the first quarter of the year 1943 he was short 70,000 men in the shipyards and couldn't get them. He will need another 150,000 before the year 1943 is over. "Yes," he admitted, "we broke all shipbuilding records in 1942, have never known anything like it, 8.2 million tons of ships, but the program for 1943 is almost 19 million tons of ships," and his great danger is that he can't find the men to do it, and there is no adequate machinery to produce them in orderly fashion.

The thing I have pleaded for from the beginning of this discussion is the orderly distribution of workers, systematic, and we can use to a very large degree the volunteer spirit.

Let me say a word about [the proposed Austin-Wadsworth] ... bill. In its first section it sets forth a fundamental principle, to the effect that every civilian adult in the United States otherwise competent and with certain liberal exemptions owes it as a duty to serve in a civilian capacity where he or she is most needed in support of the armed forces and the winning of the war.

That declaration of principle runs exactly parallel to the declaration of principle contained in the draft law which says, in effect, that every man of military age otherwise competent and not needed in a more important undertaking owes it as a duty to serve in the armed forces of the United States. There is no difference, whatsoever, my friends, between those two declarations of principle, and both are democratic, absolutely in accord with the democratic spirit. . . .

Many steps have been taken in an endeavor to cure the situation. I call to mind the condition in the copper mines. Copper is a very critical material, as you all know. We are falling down in the production of copper. There isn't any doubt about it. It is conceded we need more of it. Is it because we haven't enough copper in the ground? No, it is because we haven't got enough men mining the copper, and in a desperate endeavor to get miners for copper mines, the government, through the exercise of some mysterious power—where it comes from I do not know—ordered the closing down of all gold mines in the belief that gold miners would go to the copper mines. It just didn't happen, and we are still short of copper.

There is another side of this problem with which I come into very intimate contact, and that is the shortage of labor on the farms. The figures show that 60 per cent of all the men drained away from the land have gone to industry and 40 per cent to the armed forces. It is a curious thing that a country like the United States should be threatened as we hear with a food shortage; that is rather dismaying, disconcerting, to say the least. By comparison, you look across the ocean to England where complete mobilization of manpower has been achieved for three years, and we find that the British have so succeeded in the orderly distribution of workers in industry, in the services, and on the land, that England has increased her food production in the last three years by 50 per cent, and ours is threatening to go down by comparison. . . .

We are fighting to save ourselves from involuntary servitude. If we lose, we shall have it. We ought to employ everything we can muster to save our freedom, yes, suspend many of our rights, many of our privileges, even suspend some of our traditions, if you please, while this great war is on, but in suspending them, be conscious of the fact that when we have won it we recover them all and can live in safety and our children and our grandchildren can live in safety. It isn't involuntary servitude that we propose, nothing like it..

Is there any difference between tapping a young man on the shoulder and telling him, "Put on a uniform and go to New Guinea or North Africa and perhaps die" and tapping another civilian on the shoulder and saying, "You are needed in that factory; you will be well paid while you are there, but you are needed there to help that man in North Africa"? Surely we cannot distinguish between those two things.

THE SAME LIABILITY FOR ALL [6]

To our troops looking over their shoulders from the battlefields of the Mediterranean and the steaming jungles of the South Seas, the American front at home [as 1944 opened] suddenly seemed to be on the point of going sour. A host of what seemed to our soldiers petty controversies in industry and labor, each one of which threatened to put a check in the production of priceless weapons, arose throughout our land. The three vital industries of the home front, upon which basically all our production of weapons and transportation depend, were threatened with, or actually experienced, nationwide strikes—coal, steel, and the railroads. If such a situation had arisen in Germany, you know that we should all have thought we were on the point of winning the war hands down. . . .

I can tell you that today that situation, the industrial unrest and lack of a sense of patriotic responsibility which it seems to evidence in large numbers of our population, has aroused a strong feeling of resentment and injustice among the men of the armed forces. I believe it is hazardous to belittle the effect which such a situation will have upon the ultimate welfare of our democracy. If it continues, it will surely affect the morale of the

[6] From testimony delivered by wartime Secretary of War Henry L. Stimson before the the Senate Military Affairs Committee, January 19, 1944. *Vital Speeches of the Day.* 10:258-61. February 15, 1944. Reprinted by permission.

army. It is likely to prolong the war and endanger our ultimate success; and, when those troops come back to us again at the close of the war and we are faced with the acute problem of demobilization, it may have an effect upon the future unity of our nation which is disturbing to contemplate. This war will last much longer than [World War I]. . . . The effect of the division between the men who have borne the burden of the fighting abroad and the men who have shown this irresponsibility at home, will have a longer time to sink in and be accentuated. It will not be forgotten easily.

The men in the army see this country divided into two entirely distinct classes. On the one hand are the men who are in the armed forces. Their enlistment has been carried out with the aid of the Selective Service Law, a process of selection applied to them by their nation under the sanction of compulsion. They have been told not only that they must serve; but the time, the place, and the method of their service has been chosen for them in the light of their respective aptitudes to fit the requirements of the nation. They are facing a duty which they cannot escape and which involves the possibility of death or mutilation.

On the other side they see that the government imposes no corresponding duty upon the remaining men of the nation and even permits them to leave the most important war jobs without regard to the needs of their country.

Our democracy has been founded upon a basis of equality and justice. I tell you that today the men in the armed forces are beginning to believe that they are being discriminated against in a matter which is one of fundamental justice as between man and man. There is danger that under the influence of that feeling, they will not give even fair recognition to the tremendous production effort which has actually been accomplished by the great majority of American management and labor.

This being the situation, the evident remedy is for the nation to make clear in no uncertain terms the equality of obligation of its citizens. I have heard people say: "We must penalize strikes; it isn't necessary to pass a general service law; we must simply prevent strikes."

The trouble with this diagnosis is that it treats a symptom and not the disease. The cause of the present situation is deep and fundamental and it will not be remedied by merely making criminal what is a consequence of a grave underlying lack of responsibility.

It must be remembered that these men who strike or threaten to strike are Americans like all of the rest of us. The men in war production are not essentially different from the men who are proving themselves heroes in the South Pacific and on the Italian peninsula. They can be more accurately defined as the victims of the failure of the nation to develop a sense of responsibility in this gravest of all wars.

What we must do is to get at this underlying cause and by proper organization bring home to each of these men the fact that his individual work is just as patriotic and important to the government as any other cog in the great machine of victory; that they owe a patriotic duty to the particular job on which they are engaged comparable to that which the infantryman owes to his rifle, or the artilleryman to his gun, or the pilot to his plane.

The purpose of a national service law is to get at this basic evil which produces the irresponsibility out of which stem strikes, threats of strikes, excessive turnovers, absenteeism, and the other manifestations of irresponsibility with which we are now plagued. It is aimed to extend the principles of democracy and justice more evenly throughout our population. There is no difference between the patriotic obligations resting upon these two classes of men which I have described. Certainly the nation has no less right to require a man to make weapons than it has to require another man to fight with those weapons. Both processes should be so designated and carried out as to serve the interest of the country in winning the war. In a democracy they should also be so designed and executed as to serve the principles of justice between its citizens. . . .

I believe that a national service law will produce the following results:

First and foremost, it will minimize the calling of strikes by clarifying the patriotic duty of the individual worker. . . . This moral duty has also behind it the force of appropriate legal sanctions and penalties.

Secondly, it will remedy the grave sense of injustice which the armed forces now feel has been practiced against them. This is irrefutable and, as I have pointed out, is . . . pregnant with danger.

Thirdly, it will point out to civilian war workers that they are working for their country in the civilian ranks and that their responsibility is just as definitely recognized by the nation as that of soldiers on the front. By and large this will tend to powerfully heighten their morale in the winning of the war.

Fourthly, it will tend powerfully towards increasing effectiveness in production when the government itself takes a hand not only in keeping men on necessary jobs but also in finding men for particular jobs where they are especially needed, rather than leaving the choice to chance.

In this connection let me point out one of the greatest evils in the present situation. It is the heavy turnover of labor in some of our great war industries such as the aircraft factories. This is not only a shocking waste of manpower but it is so heavy that it stands as a constant threat to maximum production of the implements of war.

One of the important effects of the national service act would be to bring war workers from less essential to more essential industries when necessary.

At present the unevenness of the distribution of our labor is producing shortages in some of our most vital weapons when there is excess of labor available in other neighboring places. For example, while there is an excess of labor for the production of machine guns, tanks and ships in some places, in nearby places there is a shortage in the vital production of aircraft engines and landing craft.

In this situation the army has even been called upon to furlough soldiers in order that they may take the place of workmen or miners who have left their jobs to do something which they think will offer them better pay. That happened in the copper mines of Montana as well as in the airplane factories of California. Think of the waste of such a situation, taking soldiers from training for combat because they are the only persons who can be directed to stay where they are put!

On the other hand, a national service act will not cause the evils which have been feared by its opponents. The man or woman who wants to do his or her part to win the war as quickly as possible has nothing to fear from a national service act. That act does not impair the rights of the worker in respect to wage scales, hours of labor, seniority rights, membership in unions or other basic interests of the civilian workers. Wherever justified by considerations of family or health, deferment from service would be granted by the local selective service board. I would not advocate any national service act which would not protect such elemental rights to the fullest. National service acts have been enacted by the great English-speaking democracies which are now fighting this war with us, namely Great Britain, Canada, Australia, New Zealand. With them the legislation has worked so successfully that the exercise of sanctions has become rare; the existence of the national service organization and the morale which it creates having proved that the people of a country want to do their duty when it is clearly pointed out to them by their government. . . .

Our country has but one national purpose today—it is to win the war as quickly as possible. I have been discussing the logic of national service as an orderly, efficient process by which a democracy can give all-out effort in war. But more important now, national service will be the means of hastening the end of this war.

Mark what this thought really means. No variety of twisted thinking will deny the right of the millions of American men in uniform to every chance of living through this conflict. Their lives have already been placed in jeopardy by the nation in summoning them to arms. It would be an act of the most cruel and despicable indifference if we avoided any course which would give them their chance to come through this war with their lives.

We say that we can win this war. General Eisenhower has said that he believes we can win our victory over Hitler in 1944, but he has added the solemn warning that this will be possible only with the all-out effort of every American.

Every month the war is prolonged will be measured in the lives of thousands of young men, in billions of dollars. The attrition in manpower and in our national wealth will be felt for generations if this conflict is prolonged. National service is the one weapon we have neglected to use. Posterity will never forgive us if we sacrifice our plain duty to a desire for creature comfort or for private gain.

EFFECTIVE LABOR CONTROL NEEDED [7]

In the navy and the army, discipline is maintained by trained officers, working with small groups and responsible to a hierarchy of specialists activated by no other motive than duty. In civilian life, the nation's war effort [operates] . . . on the basis of relatively free choice of occupation, in work provided by employers stimulated to produce by the profit motive. Bargaining for wages and prices is not eliminated by congressional action as is the bargain for the labor of the serviceman. Those not engaged in direct war work are free to work where they choose; even those on war work who want to change their jobs can, without much difficulty, do so. . . . Supervision is in the hands of men often untrained in the subtleties of personnel administration and sometimes far from efficient. The lines of responsibility are confused and overlapping. These defects in our free enterprise system generate frictions . . . which . . . may lead to strikes. Not all strikes are for the purpose of securing wage increases; they are often the worker's expression of dissatisfaction with working conditions. While these frictions remain, strikes must be permitted as a safety valve and as a more honest alternative to a "go-slow" policy.

We condemn strikes but often because our understanding of the facts has been obscured by exaggerated publicity. During 1941, we lost one quarter of one per cent of available working time through strikes. In 1942, this rate of loss fell to less than one tenth of one per cent and, if it had not been for the coal strike, our losses in the first six months of 1943 would have been at a still lower rate. Even including the coal strike, our loss was but six tenths of one per cent. We must deplore even this small loss, especially when we realize that the costs of a strike

[7] From an address by Philip William Bishop, instructor in economics, Oberlin College, delivered at Oberlin College, January 25, 1944. Mimeographed text available from the College Publicity Bureau, Oberlin, Ohio. 1944. Reprinted by permission.

are not measured in terms of direct effects alone. Yet it seems but a small price to pay for the avoidance of the restrictions which a Hitler would know how to impose. In my judgment an honest recognition of the right to strike would do much to reduce the number and incidence of strikes.

We have no record of the time lost to our productive effort by employers' inefficiencies or by the delays caused by employers and "bureaucrats" during the negotiation of new contracts. These are taken as normal deductions from the theoretical maximum capacity of our plants and as by no means reprehensible. . . .

Till now, the allocation of our manpower has been more or less an accidental consequence of our production program. We have been working to no master plan. In consequence, we have no grounds for claiming that our use of our labor potential has been of the most efficient. We have thought too much in terms of the men actually presenting themselves for work and too little in terms of our untapped reserves. The national labor draft would provide the data for an orderly appraisal of our manpower resources and make possible a more nearly correct allocation of those resources than is possible under the voluntary system. . . . The labor draft offers an intelligent alternative to the hit and miss process by which we have achieved our present position and it offers possibilities for the active enlistment in the war effort of many who want to do their share but, as yet, have found no outlet.

It is impossible to avoid a reference to England at this point. Until the evacuation of France, she had relied on the free enterprise system to solve her production problem. The fall of France brought her near to starvation and defeat; her productive equipment was threatened with complete ruin by air raid. She turned to the labor draft and, what is more, to a wholesale reorganization of her productive lay-out, which respected the rights of none. Every resource was turned to maximum advantage and her people shifted to essential occupations almost overnight. . . .

Does this proposed labor draft threaten to undermine our basic concept of democracy? Are we reintroducing slavery of a new and more vicious kind, that of slavery to the state? Personal discipline is the essence of democracy and the American people have demonstrated this quality in high degree. Are they afraid, then, to use this discipline even to the extent of surrendering a large part of their personal initiative for the duration in return for a sense of real direction, of real implication in the war effort? Must such a surrender be a mere acceptance of totalitarianism? England has had a contrary experience. The compulsory powers under her national service act have seldom needed to be used; personal interviews with the worker selectees have resulted in voluntary adjustment to the government's plans for greater and more efficient use of their strength and skills. Given careful drafting and good administration, our own labor draft should produce . . . mass volunteering on the part of people not yet directly engaged in the war effort. In this environment we see true democracy at work. Personal discipline emphasizes the need for sacrifice.

Since the law apparently contemplates no restriction on the right to bargain for wages and conditions, it is important that these worker draftees be protected against the opportunism of employers and against attempts by badly administered trade unions to exploit the situation. Surrender of democratic rights must be coupled with full protection of democratic privileges compatible with the plan.

As to the expediency of passing a labor draft law now, my thinking has been wholly in terms of a real, present emergency. We have no means adequately to control the movement of our labor resources. We need effective labor control as much as we need effective price and wage control, and control over capital resources. That we have gone thus far without a labor draft is one of the miracles of the democratic process; but we should not continue to rely on miracles.

SACRIFICE FOR SACRIFICE'S SAKE [8]

The administration of a manpower draft would be a much more complicated task than the administration of selective

[8] From third annual report (dated March 4, 1944) of the Special Committee Investigating the National Defense Program. Report No. 10, Part 16. Superintendent of Documents. Washington, D. C. 1944. p28-30. This report is of special interest because it was submitted by Harry S. Truman, then Senator from Missouri and head of the group usually referred to as the Truman Committee.—Ed.

service, which has presented very serious problems, some of them still not completely solved. The present selective service boards clearly do not have the time, experience, and other qualifications which would be necessary to administer a national service act. Policies and procedures would have to be formulated and made known to industry, and forms would have to be prepared, circulated, filled out, returned, and classified before it would be possible to obtain even the first benefits. The time lag necessarily involved probably would be so great as to make it likely that the statute, if enacted, would not become operative for a number of months. . . . The committee does not believe that so drastic a remedy as the enactment of a manpower draft statute is warranted.

In considering such legislation it must be noted that the government, by assuming the right to determine where, in what capacity, and under what terms of employment its citizens are to work, also would be forced to assume a corresponding obligation to its citizens not only to provide employment but to provide employment at the right place, in the right occupation and at the right salary and other terms of employment, together with a further obligation to provide transportation, housing, schools, and other municipal services. These are not obligations that can be assumed lightly by any government. If they are assumed, confusion and difficulties incident to attempting to fulfill them through the many and diverse agencies which necessarily would be involved would be very great. This would be especially true during the first few months, which would be the critical period during which the proponents of the manpower draft expect to receive the greatest benefits from it.

Even the advocates of the manpower draft realize that these objections exist in addition to the fundamental objection to the regimentation of the people and the further encroachment of the military on our economy that would be involved. Many of them have stated that the principal value of the legislation would be psychological, to prevent workers from quitting present jobs. They assert that if national service legislation were enacted, it probably would be necessary to make only a few transfers of employment.

Another psychological advantage is said to be that such legislation would tend to equalize sacrifice, thereby making a contribution to service morale and increasing the determination of the civilian population to end the war so that the self-imposed sacrifice could be eliminated. This argument looks suspiciously like sacrifice for sacrifice's sake, and those making it forget that the civilians to be regimented for the sake of raising army and navy morale are the parents and relatives of the men in service, and, to the extent of over a million men, veterans who have received honorable discharges.

The argument also disregards the fact that there are few things more dangerous to success in war than war-weariness and dissatisfaction on the home front. This is particularly true of a long war. . . .

Manpower draft legislation has also been advocated as an antistrike measure, rendered necessary by the excesses of some labor groups. Unquestionably there have been excesses which are subject to the severest condemnation. However, we must not allow those excesses to obscure the fact that, on the whole, the performance by labor has been very good. Man-days of labor used for manufacturing, mining, and construction, but not including agriculture, in 1943 exceeded by 76 per cent the man-days of labor used in 1939 despite the fact that over 10 million men have been withdrawn from the labor pool for service in the armed forces. . . . If manufacturing is considered separately, man-days used in 1943 exceeded by 89.6 per cent those used in 1939. Of course, a considerable portion of these gains resulted from the reduction in unemployment, but even after making allowance for that factor, the increases are impressive.

Moreover, it should be noted also that England has had the equivalent of a manpower draft for several years and that the existence of such legislation did not preclude strikes in England. It is estimated that in the first 11 months of 1943, there were 1,638 strikes in England, involving a loss of manpower of 1,676,000 man-days. England has a population of roughly 48 million.

Comparable figures for the United States, with a population of 130 million, for the same period were 3,425 strikes involving a loss of 12,785,000 man-days. If the 823,000 man-days lost in England from coal strikes are deducted, and adjustments are made for the difference in the number of workers, our strike losses are still somewhat greater than England's. But the difference between man-days lost at our rate of strikes and man-days lost at the English rate of strikes, when compared to total man-days worked in the United States, is only 0.025 per cent.

It is doubtful whether even this percentage could be saved by enacting national service legislation. In any event, if the purpose is to reduce strikes and to regulate labor unions, that purpose could be accomplished much more efficiently by other means that would do less violence to individual freedom.

One such means would be a clear and understandable government labor-relations policy for the duration, written into law and administered through one single agency instead of the dozen or so now operating in this field. While strikes cannot be condoned, it must be stated, in fairness to organized labor, that government and management must bear their share of responsibility in varying degrees for work stoppages. When labor and management agree to government arbitration of disputes to avoid work stoppages, they are entitled to speedy decisions in accordance with clear, fair policies. This condition has not always been met. On the other hand, there have been occasions where neither management nor labor was desirous of reaching a settlement, and each has obstructed government efforts to bring about a fair settlement. . . .

Compulsion through a manpower draft should be the very last resort in a democracy such as ours, and then should be used only in very specific and well-defined areas where voluntary methods of control now available under existing law have proved inadequate.

The manpower problem is too complex and difficult to be solved by any such easy means as passing a manpower draft statute. The only way to make real progress in this field is to take up separately each of the many problems that exist and try to find means of solving or alleviating it.

NATIONAL SERVICE A HINDRANCE, NOT A HELP [9]

The first contention of the proponents of [a national service act] . . . is that it would help to solve manpower problems and to promote war production. I cannot conceive on what factual grounds that theory is based. A national service act would only substitute compulsion and regimentation for the free enterprise of American labor and American management. If we do this we will be conceding that we are wrong on the basic issues of this war and that the enemy is right. The Nazis and the Fascists believe in the totalitarian principle of slave labor and slave industry. That is their system. We in America have always believed that the free and voluntary service of our people is superior to coercion. Free enterprise is our system. . . . Enactment of this bill would constitute a catastrophic retreat and an inglorious confession of failure of the American way of life.

Have we failed? The record of this war to date [1944] proves incontestably otherwise. In the two short years since Pearl Harbor, America alone has outproduced the combined forces of the Axis by more than two to one. The facts speak for themselves. Between January 1942 and January 1944 America doubled the size of her navy by building 3.7 million displacement tons of new fighting ships. In the same period, we produced 27 million tons of merchant shipping, equal to the size of the entire world's fleet before the war. We turned out 134,000 airplanes, despite temporary shortages of materials and constantly changing designs and specifications—and we are now building the finest and most effective planes in the world at the rate of almost 10,000 a month. We have produced 148,000 tanks, 1.2 million military trucks, 424,000 pieces of artillery and more than a billion rounds of artillery ammunition.

These are the government's own figures. They add up to a production miracle—a miracle which no other country in the world can duplicate, a miracle which was accomplished through the efforts of the great army of free American workers.

[9] Testimony of William Green, President, American Federation of Labor, before the Senate Military Affairs Committee, February 16, 1944. *Vital Speeches of the Day.* 10:324-6. March 15, 1944. Reprinted by permission.

Surely this record cannot be classified as failure! On the contrary, our own allies have hailed it as the great triumph of this war. Premier Stalin, of Soviet Russia, is reported to have declared at the Teheran Conference that the United Nations would never have been able to turn the tide of battle and start the new and victorious offensives without the vast output of munitions made by American labor and American industry.

Nor is there any substantial indication that future production cannot be sustained at these high levels or even increased. On the contrary, there is abundant evidence that our country is now producing more war material in many categories than the armed forces of all the United Nations can use. . . .

I would be the last to deny that difficult manpower and production problems still confront us in some localities and in certain lines of production. The question before us, however, is whether resort to compulsion and regimentation will help us out of these difficulties or render them even greater. This is a question which the nation's leaders in the field of industry, labor and agriculture are best qualified to answer. They gave their answer last November—a unanimous answer. They declared:

> The American people will provide greater output under a voluntary system than under one of compulsion and regimentation.
> The solution depends upon leadership, coordinated and understood plans and efficient administration; not upon broadened control and regimentation.

These statements were contained in a declaration made public by the Policy Committee of the War Manpower Commission. The declaration was signed, among others, by the presidents of the United States Chamber of Commerce, the National Association of Manufacturers, the American Farm Bureau Federation, the National Grange, the National Farmers Union, the American Federation of Labor and the CIO. I repeat it was a unanimous statement; and it rejected the proposal for a national service act without qualification.

You will agree, I am sure, that it is a rare event for industry, labor and agriculture to agree on a specific policy and program which closely affects their supposedly conflicting interests and that such unanimous agreement should be given considerable weight.

It is also interesting to explore the basic cause of this agreement among the representatives of industry, labor and agriculture. It springs from their experience with the controls already put into effect by the War Manpower Commission and other government agencies. These experiences have not been happy. Instead of bringing about order, instead of simplifying procedure, instead of promoting efficiency, the record of government intervention in this field spells only confusion, red tape, contradictory policy and frustration.

Because of such experiences, the leaders of industry, labor and agriculture fear and dread the impact of utter chaos if and when a national service law is enacted and the government attempts to administer it. . . .

Now I should like to take up a new argument advanced in support of a national service act—which is, that it would help to prevent strikes. This argument also is theoretical and the theory behind it is demonstrably unsound. The only way a national service act could deal with strikes would be to place the strikers in jail, as this bill provides, for six months. But we already have a federal law, known as the War Labor Disputes Act, which provides jail penalties for strikers. The War Labor Disputes Act has not prevented strikes. Neither would a national service act.

We have only to examine the experiences of Great Britain for further confirmation. Britain has a national service law, adopted in the national emergency which followed Dunkirk. This law has not prevented strikes in Britain. On the contrary, the records show that there have been more strikes proportionately in Great Britain while the national service law was in effect there, than there have been in this country during the same period.

No one in America has been more outspoken in condemnation of wartime strikes than I have. Repeatedly I have urged the membership of the American Federation of Labor to live up to our no-strike pledge—and they have followed this advice to the extent of more than 99 per cent. There can be no possible justifications for strikes at a time when the fate of the nation and the lives of thousands of American boys hang in the balance.

But we must face the facts. Strikes have occurred and they will occur so long as the war economy of our country is out of line and out of balance. The major cause of strikes is that the government is attempting to enforce wage stabilization while it has failed to stabilize the cost of living. The way to prevent strikes is to readjust the stabilization program so that the purchasing power of the wage dollar is restored. . . .

The final argument raised in behalf of a national service act is that it would allocate the burden of war sacrifice more equitably among the American people. It is said that if the government can conscript young men to serve in the armed forces and risk their lives against the enemy, it should likewise draft those on the home front to work at the particular job and in the particular place the government deems best calculated to promote the war effort.

This argument appears plausible at first glance, but careful analysis will show that it is empty, false and irrelevant. There can be no true comparison between drafting citizens to serve in the armed forces for the defense of their country and drafting other citizens to work by compulsion in industries operating for private profit. Neither can there be any nationwide draft of labor without a correspondingly drastic draft of capital. Such measures are abhorrent to the American way of life, fatal to the free enterprise system and clearly violative of the Constitution, because they involve involuntary servitude and confiscation.

Yes, a national service act would increase the burden of sacrifice borne by those serving on the home front, but it would do so without rhyme, reason or necessity. If such a law should be enacted and strictly enforced, it is appalling to consider the fearful consequences of placing such unrestricted power in bureaucratic hands. Millions of American families might be broken up, thousands of small business enterprises might have to be abandoned. Every American citizen would be thrown into a state of uncertainty and insecurity.

Apparently, the danger of such consequences has impressed itself upon the minds of the leading supporters of this legislation, for Senator Austin declared only recently before this committee that he did not believe everyone would have to be drafted by this national service bill. He said it would only give the government the authority to draft workers when needed, just as Congress has given the government authority to seize property under certain conditions.

If this statement of the purposes of this bill by one of its authors can be relied upon, then the argument of equal sacrifice topples of its own weight. If the great majority of American citizens will be left undisturbed in their present occupations by this bill, if idlers and dilettantes and nonproductive individuals are to be permitted to pursue their own sweet way, if only certain groups of workers are to feel the brunt of enforced labor—then the idea behind a national service act is fraudulent and the burden of war sacrifice will be even more unfairly distributed than it is at present....

Our soldiers and sailors and marines who are risking their lives against enemy fire are entitled to feel that Americans at home are backing them up to the limit.

But they are also entitled to the assurance that the free America they are fighting for will be kept intact by us at home, that their homes and jobs will be protected, that they will not have to come home and be demobilized after the war ends only to be drafted for service in a job not of their own choice.

In the final analysis, the proposal for a national service act must stand or fall upon this major test—will it, or will it not, promote the war effort and hasten the day of victory? In my considered opinion, enactment of a national service law will not add a single plane, a single ship, a single tank or a single bullet to the nation's war production. On the contrary, it threatens to cripple the amazingly successful production program we are now carrying on.

UNJUSTIFIED CENTRALIZATION OF POWER [10]

We have witnessed for the past many years the centralization of power and control of the people which has been constantly

[10] From extension of remarks by Representative Charles W. Vursell, Republican of Illinois, on March 15, 1944. *Congressional Record.* 90:A1326-7. Mr. 15, '44. 78th Congress, 2d session. Reprinted by permission.

increasing year by year. Naturally, under the impact of war and the great struggle we are in, there has been less opposition to government control, because all of the people want to do everything they can do, and all of the people are willing to sacrifice and are anxious to coordinate their efforts toward the winning of the war. There has been much necessary extension of control and regimentation of the people, but under the guise of war there has been much unjustified control fastened upon them and much unjustified centralization of power.

There is a great danger in such times of stress and struggle of such controls and regimentation and centralization of power being carried entirely too far, and it is my candid opinion, and I believe the opinion of the majority of the members of this Congress, that that point will have been reached and passed if this Congress should approve and pass a national service act.

Certainly such an act should not be passed unless there is unquestioned proof that it is necessary. Certainly such an act is not in step with democracy. It is in step with the theory of a totalitarian form of government. The questions arise: Will it help to increase production of the implements of war? Will it help to increase the production of food on the farms of this country? Will it help to move more goods and materials over the transportation system of America? Will it release more manpower for the military service of our country? . . .

I have not been convinced that there is a necessity now for a national service act and I have not been convinced that such an act will lead to greater production from our mines, in our industrial plants for the winning of the war, or that it will bring any greater production from the farmers of our nation, or that it will hasten the delivery of goods over the railways or the transportation systems of our country. In fact, I fear that the passage of a national service act would retard all these endeavors which are so necessary to the well-being of the nation in these times of stress. Free men will bring forth greater production than men who are forced and regimented. . . .

I am unwilling to depart from the democracy of this country which has served it so well and embark upon such a totalitarian course unless it be proven without doubt that our manpower situation is so desperate that we must take in this country such a dangerous step in a last final effort to get the production that is necessary to win the war. And if we take this step, we are following in the very footsteps of the Nazi government which early in the war did the same thing to all of the people of [Germany]. . . .

I think the American farmers and the American workmen, all of them, whether or not they belong to any labor organization, when we take into consideration the miracle of production on the farms and in the factories that has been turned out under the democracy of this country, that they and we have demonstrated that democracy in action can be swift enough even during wartimes to maintain its democracy and at the same time develop the greatest food supply and war machine in the world. There is no question but that the men and women of this nation have not only produced the best and greatest army in the world in the shortest length of time but they have produced the greatest amount of food, munitions of war, including airplanes, tanks, trucks, guns, and battleships, of any nation in the world. And, in addition, the American people, through production and lend-lease, have sent billions of dollars' worth of farm products and of war equipment to all of the nations of the world. . . . Yet we are told we must do more, that we must draft every man and woman from the age of 18 to 65 years, and that under such a law all of these people would be at the beck and call of the government. . . . The right of workers to higher wages or their right to transfer from one job to another without permission would be denied under the law. All of them would be subject to the assignment and call of the government.

This step should not be taken. We had better look back into the history of this country and try to hold to some of the sound, fundamental principles that have made this country great. We had better be a little more proud and a little more satisfied with the accomplishments that the American men and women have been able to bring to bear in this great crisis because they have achieved miracles in production on the farms and in the mills and factories, and they have laid out their money and sent their boys throughout the world in this struggle with a devotion to this nation exemplifying as deep a patriotism as can be found in the history of any nation in the world. . . .

Forced labor and regimentation, in my judgment, will slow down production—hence, slow down the war effort. I do not believe it can be justified on any premise. . . .

Such an act will place too much power in the hands of any government.

Such an act is too far a departure from democracy in this country.

"MIRACLES OF PRODUCTION" THROUGH VOLUNTARY MEANS [11]

Our manpower program must be designed to suit the needs of a free nation, with free institutions, free traditions and democratic ways of doing things. We could make no greater mistake than to choose techniques of manpower mobilization that were incompatible with our democratic heritage and the character of our people. Our manpower program must suit the needs of a free enterprise economy that operates with the participation of free trade unions.

For four years after [World War II]. . . , I was Manpower Director for the American Military Government in Germany. The manpower program in Germany had to deal with a people that had lived under authoritarian traditions of one form or another during much of its history. German industrialists had operated in an atmosphere of government regulation and in a system of government-sanctioned trusts and controls that stifled competition. German workers had felt the perpetual presence of government coercion.

In this atmosphere of authoritarianism, German industry failed to develop the ingenuity and resourcefulness that has characterized industry in the United States. It continued to think in terms of low volume, high prices, and high-unit-profits. When times were bad it cut back on production and laid off

[11] From an address by Leo R. Wertz, Deputy Executive Director, Defense Manpower Administration, Department of Labor, before the Steel Founders Society of America, Chicago, Illinois, March 20, 1951. Mimeographed text available from the Department. Washington, D. C. 1951. Reprinted by permission.

workers, instead of stepping up its advertising and developing new markets. It went on pocketing the profits instead of plowing them back into expansions and improvement.

German labor became sluggish. Its productivity was low. Its organizations lacked the dynamic qualities that labor unions have shown in the United States. The effects of Hitlerism had made German labor poorly equipped to assume a leading role in the reconstruction of the country.

The very qualities that have been lacking in Germany, the United States has had in abundance. In an atmosphere of freedom, industry and labor in the United States have developed an initiative and a resourcefulness that are unmatched anywhere in the world. After four years in Europe, I can tell you how significant those qualities are. It would be tragic if we failed to make full use of them in the mobilization program that is ahead.

To suit the United States and its people, our manpower program must be a voluntary program. It must be based upon the consent and participation of the workers and employers who will be affected by it. We are not going to try to regiment anybody. To do that would be to stifle the initiative, the ingenuity and the creative genius that have made this country great. We know that America's miracles of production were not accomplished through regimentation. We can force the worker to stand at his work bench or the boss to keep his plant running, but we cannot force either to use his full capacity for production. That must come from his own free determination to serve our national purpose. . . .

A voluntary program means participation by labor and management. That is the heart and soul of it, the thing that makes it suit our democratic temperament. It is labor-management participation that has been the dominant idea of Maurice J. Tobin, the Secretary of Labor, ever since President Truman assigned his department the job of mobilizing manpower.

At the heart of the Labor Department's manpower program is a national management-labor advisory committee. This committee advises on national policy. Labor-management participation goes farther than that, however. We are establishing labor-management committees in all of the 13 regions of the country and in every major industrial center in the United States. There will be more than 150 committees covering the major areas.

The idea is to let labor and management—the two groups most affected by manpower mobilization—have a big share in shaping the program. Most manpower problems, as I have indicated, will be local problems. They will be solved by the labor and management groups working together with government at the local level. Local problems will thus be solved by local people, the people best equipped to deal with them.

If the defense program were to change radically, it might be necessary to develop some additional techniques for manpower mobilization, techniques that are not presently contemplated. If that were to happen, however, labor and management would participate in deciding what the techniques were, whether they were really needed, and when they should be applied.

No manpower program in the United States can succeed without the overwhelming support of labor and management.... It is one thing for the government to call on workers and employers to make sacrifices for the defense program. That part is easy. It is another thing to instill in workers and employers the understanding and the confidence and the sense of participation in the defense program so that they will obey the call. "Will they come when you call them?" That will be the big test in the days that are ahead.

I have no doubt what the answer will be. Our program rests on the theory that people do things better and more quickly when they've chosen to do them themselves and when they know why. This theory, of course, is in direct conflict with the philosophy of the totalitarian world that man must be regimented if he is to perform efficiently.

The struggle, then, is a struggle between free manpower mobilized by voluntary means, and slave manpower mobilized by totalitarian coercion. The challege is to prove that our free and voluntary way is a better way than the way of the dictators.

NATIONAL SERVICE IN WARTIME BRITAIN [12]

The [British] Government's decision to introduce a measure of compulsory training in the armed forces of the Crown for men between the ages of 20 and 21 was announced . . . on April 26, 1939, and was given statutory effect by the Military Training Act which received the Royal assent on May 26. The Act, which was to have a duration of three years, placed a liability to be registered in the military training register on all male British subjects ordinarily resident in Great Britain while they were between the ages of 20 and 21. All men registered in the military training register were liable during the period of one year from the date of their registration to be medically examined and to be called up for a special course of training in the armed forces.

Men called up were deemed to be enlisted as militiamen under Section 30 of the Territorial and Reserve Forces Act, 1907, and had a total liability of four years' service of which a continuous period of six months had to be spent in full-time training with the forces. Men expressing a preference for navy or air force training were to be given a reasonable opportunity of entering the service of their choice on terms involving a continuous period of not less than six months' training.

The only persons specifically exempted from the scope of the Act, apart from the mentally defective and the blind, were men employed in the service of a dominion or colonial government, men serving in the regular forces and those who, before April 27, 1939, had already contracted a liability for service in any of the reserve or auxiliary forces. Provision was, however, made for the granting of postponement of liability to be called up on grounds of hardship, if good cause were shown, or, similarly, for permission to be given to be registered in the military training register before attaining the age of 20, and for men claiming to be conscientious objectors to make application for their cases to be considered by appropriate tribunals. The Act also provided safeguards for reinstatement in civil employment at the termination of the period of training.

[12] From *Report for the Years 1939-1946* (Cmd. 7225), by the British Ministry of Labor and National Service. His Majesty's Stationery Office. London. 1947. p8-13, 35-8. Reprinted by permission.

Only one group registration was effected under the Military Training Act. This took place on June 3, 1939, at local offices of the Ministry of Labor and related to all men who at that date were between the ages of 20 and 21. Each man registered was asked to furnish necessary personal particulars including date of birth, an exact description of his occupation, and the name and address of his employer.

Immediately after the outbreak of war the Military Training Act was superseded for the duration of the "present emergency" by the National Service (Armed Forces) Act, 1939. . . . This Act provided authority for the making of Royal Proclamations imposing liability for service with the armed forces on men in any age group between the limits of 18 and 41.

The Act applied, with certain exceptions, to British subjects who were within Great Britain at the date on which a proclamation was made relating to their particular age group or who subsequently entered the country. Men already registered under the Military Training Act were deemed to be registered under the new Act and their liability to be called up for training was superseded by a liability to be called up for service for the duration of the "present emergency." The classes of persons excluded from the scope of the Act were substantially the same as those excluded by the Military Training Act with the addition of men in holy orders and regular ministers of any religious denomination. The Act made provision for registration as a conscientious objector, for postponement of call-up on account of exceptional hardship and for reinstatement in employment after a period of service in the forces. . . .

The National Service Act, 1941, . . . made provision for the calling up of men for civil defense, and in addition made some minor amendments in the National Service (Armed Forces) Act, 1939.

The National Service (No. 2) Act, 1941, . . . imposed on all persons of either sex a general obligation for service in the armed forces, civil defense, industry, or otherwise; thus, for the first time in [British] . . . history, extending conscription to include women.[13] It demonstrated the determination of the gov-

---

[13] See selection in next section on women in wartime Britain.—Ed.

ernment that there should be complete mobilization for war; and, because it was accepted by the public without demur, it demonstrated equally the will to win of the whole country.

In addition, the Act extended the upper age limit of liability for service in the armed forces to persons up to the age of 51. Another important provision enabled the Minister [of Labor and National Service] to call up for service any person who had been discharged from any of the armed forces or civil defense without the necessity of awaiting a further proclamation. . . . Men who had been discharged on medical grounds were not to be called up for further service.

The National Service Act, 1942, . . . reduced to 17 years and 8 months the age at which men could be called upon to register, although the age at which a man became liable to be called up for service in the armed forces continued to be 18. . . .

The Ministry [of Labor and National Service] was engaged from 1937 onwards in the compilation of a Schedule of Reserved Occupations [Deferments], to come into operation in the event of war, for the purpose of determining what age-classes of men in the occupations specified in the Schedule should *not* be withdrawn from civil employment for recruitment to the services. The Schedule was prepared after careful estimates had been made of the supply of skilled men of the many different types that would be of importance in wartime and of the probable demand for such labor for war production, for the maintenance of the necessary civilian services, and for tradesmen's jobs in the armed forces. . . . . .

On September 3, 1939, the wartime schedule came into force. The main difference between the peacetime and the wartime schedules was in the principles of their application. Under the peacetime schedule men were eligible to join the national defense services in their trade or professional capacity, irrespective of age. Under the wartime schedule, men at or above the age specified for each occupation were in general ineligible for acceptance in any capacity into the armed forces or for full-time civil defense work; and men in prescribed occupations were accepted for service only in their trade capacity, except where the number of men below the reservation age was in excess of the number required as service tradesmen. . . .

The main problems which arose in the mobilization of labor for industry were: (a) the control, supply and distribution of the available skilled, semiskilled and unskilled labor; (b) securing the most effective use of labor, particularly highly skilled and heavy male labor and mobile female labor; (c) training workers to increase the supply of skilled and semiskilled labor. . . .

The demands for labor for the expanding war industries could at first be met from the unemployed and other reserves of manpower and by the attraction of workpeople from the less essential industries. The fall of France in May 1940 profoundly altered the situation. Apart from the increased demand for labor to meet the immediate needs of defense against the threatened invasion of [Britain] . . . it was necessary to formulate and put into operation long-term plans for the use of the whole of the nation's labor force.

On May 22, 1940, the Minister [of Labor and National Service] took drastic powers of control over labor under the Emergency Powers (Defense) Acts, 1939 and 1940. By Regulation 58A powers were taken to direct men and women to particular employments. In June 1940 the Restriction of Engagement Order was made (a) to stop the dislocation of employment in the engineering and building and civil engineering industries due to the poaching of labor by inducements of bonuses and high wages, and (b) to conserve the labor supply in agriculture and coal mining by stopping the drift of labor from those industries into the more highly remunerated munitions industries. From March 1941 the Essential Work Orders restricted the right of employers to discharge workpeople and of workpeople to leave employment, and so prevented excessive turnover of labor. The main lines of the controls had now been determined, although there were some later extensions, and in 1942, the increasing numbers of women entering industry led to the Control of Engagement Orders for women. . . .

The use of the Schedule of Reserved Occupations and an orderly calling up for military service by age groups were parts of a plan formulated before the war for ensuring that essential industries and services retained an adequate labor force. After May 1940 the need to recruit and equip a much larger military force than had previously been contemplated intensified the problem of the proper distribution in the national interest of the limited supply of manpower available. . . .

The expansion of the munitions industries, together with the demands of the forces and of civil defense, increased the calls on the reserves of labor, which consisted principally of the unemployed, the "non-industrial" classes and men and women above normal working age. . . . By mid-1941 the reserves of men had been exhausted. Large numbers of women had also been absorbed into industry and it became increasingly necessary to rely on women for building up the war industries. The further mobilization of women was effected by the Registration for Employment Order, 1941. In April of that year the Ministry began the registration for employment of men above military age up to age 50 to ensure that such men were being employed to the best advantage in the national interest. In the same month the registration of women was begun and by October 1942 had extended to include women aged 18 to 45. Registration was followed by interview and, if necessary, direction to work.

In 1942 the supply of single women for industry was becoming exhausted, and it was necessary to bring in many married women, many of whom had household responsibilities. This resulted in a wide extension of part-time employment. The increasing stringency in the labor supply position and the heavy labor demands in 1943 for the aircraft industry, which during the summer had the first call on all labor becoming available, led to the registration for employment of women up to age 50. . . .

The economical use of labor depended mainly on the energy and initiative of employers, but to assist in stimulating the breaking down of highly skilled work into less skilled operations, the

Minister appointed in July 1940 a number of Labor Supply Inspectors with technical experience. It was their duty to consider whether employers' demands for additional workers were justified and to secure the release of skilled men for transfer to work of greater importance than that on which they were engaged. The release and transfer of skilled men was carried out in cooperation with the Government Supply Departments. It was also the duty of the inspectors to examine the way in which skilled workers were being used, to advise how processes could be subdivided and simplified, to stimulate the training of workers in employers' establishments or in training centers supervised by the Ministry, and to encourage upgrading and the employment of semiskilled and unskilled men and women to the greatest possible extent.

WARTIME MANPOWER CONTROLS IN JAPAN [14]

In 1937 Japan began its all-out mobilization for war, although some provisions of the laws passed at that time were not actually enforced until after Pearl Harbor. The authorities realized that they would need a more thorough control over national resources, including manpower. The labor force was still largely engaged in normal peacetime pursuits, the bulk of them in agriculture. It was therefore necessary to set up national sanctions which would serve to channel labor into important war industries and to mobilize portions of the labor force not fully utilized, such as females; also to try to get more effort and more efficiency out of the existing workers in essential industries. The measures adopted constituted a progressive series designed to "scrape the barrel" nearer and nearer to the bottom.

The Employment Exchange Law of 1921 was amended in 1938 with a view to tightening government control over recruitment and placement of labor. No new private employment agencies were to be authorized and those then in existence would be strictly regulated by the government. Also, under the revised

[14] From an article by Edgar C. McVoy, United States Department of the Army, Tokyo. *American Sociological Review*. 15:534-45. August 1950. Reprinted by permission.

law, the public employment exchanges were brought, to a large extent, under national regulation, although technically they were still locally administered. The revisions in the Employment Exchange Law also provided a control over recruitment of labor by private individuals and over the supply of labor by labor bosses.

In 1938 the Diet passed the National Mobilization Law which concerned all aspects of the nation's activities but had specific articles applying to employment and labor. These articles had the following provisions . . . :

1. Authority for the government to draft labor for industrial service, implemented by an Imperial Ordinance in 1939.

2. Mobilization of special groups for national labor service. These groups included students, women's groups and patriotic organizations. Ostensibly, they volunteered to do war service for the nation but actually there were compulsory controls over their activities, especially in the later war years. In addition to students, there were two patriotic labor associations: one composed of regular workers and the other composed of casual workers under labor bosses. Both groups were used by the government during the war as a means of mobilizing labor. This regulation was enforced in December 1941.

3. Control over placement, discharge and quitting by workers, enforced in January 1942. The effect of this regulation was to freeze labor in essential jobs and to control the hiring of new workers in the interests of war production. A related provision, which was enforced in 1938, concerned the control and use of school graduates and technicians.

4. National Job Qualification Report. By Imperial Ordinance of January 1939 all skilled workers were required to file with the government a statement of education and experience to show types of work for which they were suited. This was used as a means of directing labor into necessary jobs.

In addition to the provisions of the National Mobilization Law, there were other laws passed during the war which had direct effect in controlling labor. Among these were the National Labor Notebook Law which required every skilled or semiskilled worker to carry a notebook showing the record of his employment. This was passed in March 1941. There was also the Industrial Mobilization Law of 1943 which provided for government control over business firms, including their hiring and use of labor, and the Factory and Workshop Ordinance of 1944,

UNIVERSAL CONSCRIPTION 143

which set up military ranks in munitions factories and accompanying military discipline, including saluting. . . .

The major agency for enforcement (other than the omnipresent police) was the euphemistically named Welfare Ministry, which was created in 1938. One of its major functions was labor control, although it dealt also with sanitation, health, social insurance and other matters. Locally, this Ministry operated through prefectural governors and through them to the public employment exchanges, for control of placement of workers. A history of the name applied to these exchanges during the war is indicative of their function. The traditional name of the public employment exchange is *Shokugyo Shokai Sho* or Employment Introduction Place. In 1941 the name was changed to *Kokumin Shokugyo Shido Sho* or National Employment Guidance Place. In 1944 the name was changed to *Kokumin Kinro Doin Sho* or National Diligent Labor Mobilization Place.

The methods of mobilizing labor were different for four major groups of the labor force, as described below:

1. *Skilled labor and technicians.* The manager of a munitions plant would send to the Munitions, War or Navy Ministry a request for a certain number of skilled workers of given types. This request would be considered by a committee representing several ministries, although the most influential were the Munitions, Navy, War and Welfare Ministries. The committee would decide whether the request could be filled in view of the national manpower situation. Having been approved by the committee, the request was turned over to the Welfare Ministry, which consulted its records on skilled labor registration to determine what prefectures had the required labor available. Welfare Ministry then would send a quota to several prefectures for filling this requirement. The next step was for the Prefectural Employment Exchange Unit of the Education Section (after November 1942 under the Police Section) acting for the Prefectural Governor, to select names of workers from their prefectural roster. The list of names would then be sent to local employment exchanges for enforcement.

The local office would deliver a "white card" to the worker and instruct him to appear at the office on a certain day. When he arrived he would be told what job he would be sent to. This was likely to be in a different prefecture or a distant location. Ordinarily, the worker accepted his assignment without protest; this was partly because of a powerful barrage of propaganda which had been streaming from Tokyo for years, concerning the duty of each Japanese to the emperor. However, in case the patriotic appeal was not enough, the man could be fined up to one thousand yen or imprisoned for a year for violation of these regulations. Actually, there were few cases of non-compliance and almost no instances of prosecution over this provision.

This does not mean that workers gladly accepted conscription. It only means that there was, other than a few cases where political influence was used to avoid conscription, no practical alternative to compliance, because of local pressures to conform and close police surveillance of individual conduct. There are some cases reported of "white card" labor draftees being sent to factories away from home, and, upon being granted leave to return home for a short time, refusing to return to the factory....

The basic method of control, not only for manpower regulations, but for all purposes by the government, was through propaganda and through the military and civil police, who were instructed to watch for disaffection of any type. Any dissenters with the national policy were dealt with severely. Such dissension might concern any policies for mobilization or conduct of the war, as well as willingness to enter into national industrial service.

2. *Casual labor.* In this case the manager of the munitions plant would send his request directly to the local employment office. If this office could fill the request locally that was the end of the matter. (Incidentally, local recruitment was done through labor bosses.) If there was not enough labor available locally, they would send a request to another area, and with the cooperation of the casual laborers' patriotic organization, would obtain the labor from another area. If they still could not get enough labor, the government would ask the other labor patriotic groups,

who would then organize a group of students or other special workers to handle the job.

3. *Special groups.* This was composed primarily of students and women. From the school records appropriate workers were selected for various purposes, either for common labor in industry or for harvest work in agriculture. A great deal of patriotic drum beating was done, and it was tacitly understood that no one would refuse to serve, although ostensibly everything was on a voluntary basis.

Mobilization of students was started in 1939 as vacation work on farms, but was extended in 1941 to work on farms even during the school term, and in 1943 to work in factories. By 1944, many factories had become dependent on students for a substantial portion of their labor force, and education was considered as of minor importance. At its peak, student employment reached about three million.

There were also progressive drives to increase the number of women in employment, both in agriculture and industry. From 1930 to 1940, the major trend was an increase of females in agriculture to offset the movement of males to industry and the armed forces. From 1940 to 1944, the proportion of females increased not only in agriculture, but in fishing, mining, commerce, transportation, government, and all categories except manufacturing and construction.

4. *Korean and foreign labor.* Koreans were considered as Japanese nationals subject to the same laws. However, for the most part they were mobilized on "voluntary contract" basis. A Japanese company, usually a mining company, would be authorized to recruit labor from Korea. The company representative would go to Korea and would engage workers who were sent to Japan and organized into gangs. During the war, in any of the industries considered essential, such as coal and metal mining, workers were not permitted to leave their employment during the term of thir contract. Most of the enforcement was done by company guards with the sanction of the police. The net result was a condition of virtual slave labor. Chinese coolies were recruited and employed on the same basis as Koreans, with the

exception of prisoners of war, who were forced to work under guard. From 1939 to 1945, 166,000 Korean contract workers were brought to Japan.

Penalty for leaving employment to which a person had been assigned in the national interest was the same as for refusing to accept the assignment in the first place: that is, a maximum of one thousand yen or one year's imprisonment. Again there were few cases that came to a point of prosecution because of the other sanctions applied.

THE ROLE OF WOMEN

OUR GREAT UNUSED RESOURCE—
WOMANPOWER [1]

In [World War II] ... we overcame prejudice and tradition to the extent of inviting women into all branches of the service. The importance of the army and navy nurse corps had long been established, but there was widespread opposition to women in the armed forces in any other capacity. Recruitment was slow, partly because the first public reaction was to criticize and ridicule the women who volunteered; indeed, we never completely succeeded in putting across the idea that women were really needed and wanted in the armed forces.

In the beginning, women were allowed to perform only the simplest and least responsible military tasks, but by the close of the war their range of duties had greatly increased and they had convinced even the most skeptical of their competence and seriousness of purpose. The fact that women have now been given a permanent place in the regular army, navy, air force and marine corps is evidence of the success with which those first volunteers met a triple test: learning new jobs; proving that they could do those jobs without special favors; and convincing their families and the public that they were rendering an essential service. ...

The groundwork is already laid for women to carry a large share of military duties in the event of a national emergency. The ... women now on active duty constitute a nucleus for the training and discipline of new recruits in large numbers. Thousands of those who had training and experience in World War II could be reenlisted and reassigned quickly. Most important of

---

[1] From an article by Dorothy C. Stratton, director of the SPARS (women's branch of the United States Coast Guard) in World War II and presently director of the Girl Scouts of the United States of America. New York *Times Magazine*. p 17+. October 1, 1950. Reprinted by permission.

all, there is a great deal less resistance in all quarters to military service for women.

The simple statement that the number of women in the United States labor force rose from around 13 million in 1940 to 19 million at the peak of wartime employment in 1944 needs no elaboration to indicate the contributions of women on civilian jobs. Although some of this increase was accounted for by occupations traditionally open to women, such as agricultural, clerical, stenographic, or sales work, the largest growth, both numerically and percentagewise, took place in the occupation group which the Bureau of the Census labels "craftsmen, foremen, operatives and laborers except farm."

In industry, also, women were met at first with apathy or outright resistance. The reluctance of employers grew out of their assumptions that women had no mechanical aptitude, were not accustomed to the discipline of regular working hours and close supervision and would not be able to work side by side with men without disrupting plant morale.

As the number of women on the production lines began to rise after Pearl Harbor, plant officials learned that many of their fears had been groundless. The Women's Bureau of the Department of Labor, which conducted a long-range survey of aircraft assembly plants during the prewar and war periods, was able to report that even in the early part of 1942 "some of the foremen who had expressed a presumptive opposition to the induction of women in their sections were among the most effusive in their praise of the quality and quantity of the work done by women under their supervision, and were even willing to admit its equality to that of men."

Certain real difficulties had to be met. Some modifications were necessary in personnel practices and physical plant facilities that had been designed originally for all-male factory forces. Women who would not have been in the labor force except for the war found difficulty in working out a schedule which included both home and job responsibilities.

The total employment of women on actual production jobs in manufacturing reached its peak in the late fall of 1943, when

4.8 million women constituted 32.2 per cent of all workers in this field. There were 478,000 women in the aircraft industry alone; they made up 36.5 per cent of the production force, as against a mere fraction of one per cent in 1940. Women learned to do highly skilled jobs in precision assembly and in the machine shops of aircraft plants. In the making of electrical machinery and equipment, a light industry which had employed women on almost a third of its production jobs before the war, the number of women rose to 370,000 (48 per cent).

The shipbuilding industry, in which a number of the jobs are physically difficult, disagreeable, or dangerous, was understandably slow to admit women, yet in October 1943 there were 164,700 women (9.6 per cent) in the shipyards. Many of them worked outdoors in all kinds of weather; some worked on high scaffolding; others even cleaned bilge or did sandblasting on ships in drydock. In iron and steel, another heavy industry that was reluctant to employ women, the number of women in the plants continued to climb until the autumn of 1944, when the total stood at 381,600 (22.3 per cent).

Since these facts and figures are recent history, it is not unreasonable (though perhaps it is overly optimistic) to expect that industry as a whole has advanced to the point of accepting women as desirable employees in their own right, not merely as substitutes for men.

The activities of women in volunteer agencies were as vital to the success of the war effort as they are to the peacetime life of communities. Particularly for women who have family responsibilities, these agencies, with their trained professional leadership, offer an organized means of using part-time services effectively. The unregimented and unselfish efforts of women in World War II, whether in civilian defense, the Red Cross, USO and youth-serving organizations or on rationing boards, demonstrated the strength and effectiveness of the womanpower which can be mobilized through volunteer groups in our communities.

In order to take advantage of the progress that has already been made toward the most effective use of our nation's womanpower, we need to think straight about a number of basic principles. First of all, women must be accepted as full partners. In order to give their best effort, they must believe that they are needed and wanted and that their contribution is respected. We cannot expect women to respond with enthusiasm unless they are given the opportunity to serve at every level of responsibility —from the assembly line to top planning. Planning brains are not distributed on the basis of sex any more than is skill at riveting.

We need to rid ourselves of such easy clichés as: "Women are undisciplined"—"Women can't take supervision"—"Women don't like to work for other women"—"Women are poor executives." Generalizations about women are no more valid than generalizations about men, Latin Americans, college students, or Democrats.

The approach used in asking women to serve is also important. We must accept the fact that modern warfare knows no sex differences. Women themselves know this and will respond more readily to serious appeals on an adult basis than to the inducements of glamour, adventure and novelty.

We cannot lose sight of the fact that women have special family responsibilities which cannot be neglected even in a period of stress. To hire women for war production and in the process to damage the next generation irreparably would be shortsighted and foolish. When we speak of planning for the maximum employment of women we mean women who can be spared from urgent family responsibilities.

In planning for the full participation of women in national mobilization, we have to know what are the jobs that need to be done, who is available to do them and how we are going to recruit the women needed for them. The responsibility of determining the kinds of jobs that will need to be done and the number of workers that will be required rests largely with government and industry. The analysis of jobs should not begin with the a priori assumption that certain jobs per se are men's jobs. The last war taught us that women can learn to do almost any job within their physical capacities.

Of course not every woman can learn to do every job. Selective placement is as important for women as it is for men.

People are not much happier in an emergency than in times of peace doing jobs for which they are unsuited by training, experience and aptitude. We need counseling and testing by trained advisers if we are not to waste our human talent.

As an example of the efforts presently being made to extend the scope of the assignments open to women, the air force has been conducting an experiment within the past few months to find out which of the new postwar jobs in aviation can be done by women. If we begin now, before the pressure for production becomes too great, similar programs of trial placements for women in many areas of work should yield valuable results.

In order to find out what women we have to do the jobs, we need an inventory of our resources. This inventory should include information as to family dependents, age, marital status, education, experience and special skills. The upper age limit should be rather high, perhaps 60, because many women above the age of 50 tend to be more free of family duties than younger women and could serve in numerous civilian capacities in their home communities.

The usefulness of such a registration might be gauged by trying it out in selected communities. In addition to indicating that women's abilities were being regarded seriously, it would be revealing in a number of ways. It would tell us how many women in the selected samplings were free from family responsibility and how many already had special training and skills. It would give us an indication of the willingness of women to register for service. It would also tend to prepare the nation psychologically for the registration of women on a large scale. After we have an estimate of the kinds of jobs that need to be done and the womanpower we have for them, we can find out where there are gaps and prepare at once to start training to fill them.

Our third problem, that of how we are going to get the women needed for the jobs, is one that is already emotionally charged. Any discussion of this matter sooner or later comes to the question: "In the event of national emergency, would we draft women?" The answer to this question is not simple. In the last war Great Britain drafted women between the ages of

18 and 50 without dependents under 14 for industry, the land army and the armed forces. At the peak of the war effort British women made up 33 per cent of the labor force and about 10 per cent of the armed forces.[2] In this country, on the other hand, relying entirely on voluntary recruitment of women, we brought the percentage of women in the labor force up to 30 per cent, but were able to enlist women for only 2 per cent of the armed forces.

Unless our needs should be significantly greater than before, it may be possible to get the women needed for civilian jobs without compulsion. The situation with regard to the armed forces is different, however. The problem of recruiting women for military duty is made difficult by a number of specific requirements over and above those for civilian jobs. First of all, the armed forces require mobility; women must be available to serve wherever ordered. This means in effect that women with dependents are excluded; and, in fact, the services do not now accept women with dependents under the age of 18.

A second requirement is enlistment for the period of the emergency. Many women hesitate to make this kind of open-ended commitment unless required to do so. In addition to age limitations and educational qualifications, the services also have high physical requirements. Our experience of the last war indicates that many women within the prescribed age limits cannot meet the service requirements and that of those who can, only a small percentage will do so voluntarily.

When the demands of the armed services are weighed against the advantages of staying at home and earning high wages on a civilian job, the civilian job often wins. Moreover, many young women take the position that if the nation should really need them in the armed forces it would draft them. They consider that there is no more reason why they should be exempt from compulsory service than their brothers and husbands. They accept such a possibility with more equanimity than their elders, many of whom are violently opposed to the idea. . . .

During World War II, the entire number of women in all the armed services [totaled] . . . just about one fourth of the

[2] See next selection on British women in World War II.—Ed.

number that the army estimated it could have used. The quotas in a future emergency would undoubtedly be higher. If another crisis should come, we would in all probability try first to recruit women on a voluntary basis. If this method should fail to produce the numbers needed, the only course open to us would be some form of compulsory service. Whether this would include industry or be restricted to the armed forces would depend upon the scope of the plan in effect for men.

In a struggle for survival, surely we can put aside thinking in our familiar dichotomies: man-woman, single-married, Christian-Jew, black-white, and labor-management. We are all expendable. The questions are only "Where?" and "In what capacity?"

WOMEN IN WARTIME BRITAIN [3]

Women in industry: . . . Previous to the spring of 1940, the supply of labor [in Britain] was fairly adequate, but after the fall of France an urgent need arose for more manpower. As the reserves of men were exhausted, women became the sole additional labor supply on which to draw if the war industries were to run at maximum production. In response to this need, women poured into the war industries. More than two million women entered industry between 1939 and 1943 [rising to 39 per cent of the total work force in 1943]. . . .

Power to direct men and women to employment had been given the Minister of Labor and National Service in Regulation 58-A of the Emergency Powers (Defense) Act, 1940. This was sufficient authorization for registering women and directing them to work. Such registration began in April 1941 and from April 1941 until November 1943 women between 18 and 50 years of age were registered on a semimonthly basis. This registration supplied information on the number and geographic distribution of women according to certain broad categories such as degree of home responsibility. It thus provided a survey of the avail-

---

[3] From *The Role of Women in Wartime Britain (1939-45)*, prepared by Margaret M. Fitzpatrick, of the Research Division, Women's Bureau, Department of Labor. The Bureau, Washington, D.C. 1950. p3-11. Reprinted by permission.

able labor supply, indicated whether those already employed were in essential work, and supplied a quick means for discovering which women were "mobile" and could be used to fill vacancies in industries outside the local area.

Although all women in the specified age groups were required to register, not all were called for the selection interviews, the next procedural step. In the early period of mobilization, numerous groups were exempted. Later on, as the manpower shortages grew even more acute, postponements and exemptions were reduced to a minimum. After the selection interview, if a woman was declared available, she was classified as "mobile" or "immobile." The first category included single women 19 to 45 years of age with no household responsibilities. The latter category encompassed married woman living with their husbands or with husbands in the armed forces or merchant navy, women over 45, women under 19, single women and widows with important household responsibilities. . . .

Mobilization of single women did not provide the numbers sufficient to meet the manpower demands and it was necessary in 1942 to make plans for the inclusion of married women. They were called up for interview and, where their circumstances would permit, issued directions to employment. Later in the same year, because total mobilization of women was absolutely essential, the use of direction to part-time work was introduced. Part-time work was not restricted to war industry alone but included all jobs which could be organized on a part-time basis. In this way, full-time workers were released for jobs which could only be done on a full-time basis.

Control of women did not stop with their mobilization, but covered their movement in the labor force. Having placed them in jobs, it was necessary that they be kept in them as long as they were needed. Manpower control legislation was made equally applicable to men and women. The controls included obtaining government approval before leaving a job in an essential industry, securing employment only through the government Employment Exchange and notification to the government by employers of any termination or prospective termination of employment.

Although severe and far-reaching, the controls were accepted. They were generally recognized as necessary and a system of appeal from them was provided for both worker and employer. Also, questioning by members of Parliament demanded explanation from the government in instances of careless or overbearing application of the controls. In addition, manpower policy was kept under constant review and modifications were made as they appeared to be necessary. . . .

Women in the Armed Forces: Just as the employment of women in industry was not new for Great Britain, the presence of women in an auxiliary capacity in the armed forces was also not an innovation. In World War I, over a hundred thousand women had been recruited for the various auxiliary services which, after the war, were completely disbanded. In the early 1930s, however, a group of ex-service women formed a small voluntary organization for the purpose of preparing a nucleus of officer candidates around which a new force could be created in case of emergency. This group was formally recognized by the government in 1936 and given the official name of Emergency Service. Instructors from the men's regular services gave basic training to about four hundred women and camps for women volunteers were organized during 1937-1938. Back of this was the government's decision to substitute women for men in noncombatant duties in the fighting services.

As the possibility of war became more definite, the government established three auxiliary services for women: the Auxiliary Territory Service in 1938 and, in 1939, the Women's Auxiliary Air Force and the Women's Royal Naval Service. Women directors were placed at the head of each of the auxiliary services—all of them drawn from the group of prime movers in the Emergency Service.

In the first years of the war, recruitment for these services was on a voluntary basis. But as the shortage of personnel in the armed forces became acute it was decided to conscript women for the Auxiliary Services to release men for active duty. Consequently, in December 1941, the National Service (Armed

Forces) Act was extended to include women. By this act, single women and childless widows between the ages of 20 and 30 years [amended in 1943 to include 19 year olds] were made liable for military service or other form of national service. Exemption was granted to women already enrolled in the women's services, married women, and women with children of their own under 14 years of age living with them. When called up, women were given a choice between entering (a) the Women's Auxiliary Services, (b) the civil defense forces, and (c) vital war work specified by the Minister of Labor and National Service. After a time the option for civil defense was withdrawn and, in January 1944, the option for the Women's Auxiliary Services was also suspended because of the shortage of mobile women for industry.

While no Schedule of Reserved Occupations [4] was formally drawn up for women, a list was made of industries and services important to the war effort which in practice "reserved" women and exempted them from call-up. Women not reserved could seek deferment if it was deemed to be in the national interest that they should not be moved from their work. Women were given the same right as men to plead conscientious objection, to claim deferment on the grounds of extreme hardship, and to be reinstated to civilian employment upon discharge. . . .

The Women's Auxiliary Services (ATS, WRNS, and WAAF) grew from a modest number in 1939 to a combined total of 467,000 in the summer of 1944, the period of largest membership. At this time, approximately 10 per cent of the armed forces consisted of women. . . .

Women in Civil Defense: . . . In March 1937 the Air Raid Precautions Department asked for 300,000 volunteer air raid wardens. It was taken for granted that men would fill these posts, although no one advanced any basic reason why women should not perform the duties. The next year saw the issuance of a call for an additional million volunteers. Now, women began to take over such duties as air raid wardens, ambulance drivers, clerks and storekeepers, and duties in first aid posts and

---

[4] See selection on national service in Britain in previous section.—Ed.

report centers. In London, the fire brigade opened certain classes in its organization to women.

Mobilization of women passed through the same phase in civil defense as it did in the armed forces and industry. That is, it began on a voluntary basis and shifted later, under the pressure of manpower shortages, to a compulsory basis for both full- and part-time work. . . . Disciplinary penalties were imposed on members if they disobeyed any order given them in the course of their employment or if they were absent from duty without reasonable excuse.

Women served in all the civil defense forces—general services, National Fire services, Fire Guard, Royal Observer Corps, Navy, Army and Air Force Institutes, Women's Auxiliary Police Force, Home Guard Auxiliaries, and Air Transport Auxiliary. In these various organizations women performed a variety of duties frequently dangerous and sometimes resulting in death. . . .

Women composed a substantial portion of the civil defense forces throughout the war, constituting well over a fifth of the civilian defense forces in 1943.

SHOULD WOMEN BE DRAFTED FOR MILITARY SERVICE? [5]

No one doubts the usefulness of women in uniform. World War II proved it, through the magnificent work at home and overseas of the 250,000 young women in the Women's Army Corps, the WAVES, the women marines, and the SPARS (Coast Guard). But all these women were volunteers.

Today the draft of men is moving into more and more homes. Up to now, Uncle Sam has been calling single men between 19 and 25. But there's talk about raising the draft age to 35, taking young fathers, and putting World War II veterans back into uniform. As these swift-moving events develop, more and more people are considering both sides of the question: Should Uncle Sam have the power to draft women for military service?

[5] From "Should Uncle Sam Draft Women?" by Herbert L. Marx, Jr., associate editor of *Scholastic Magazines. Senior Scholastic.* 57:18-19. September 27, 1950. Reprinted by permission of Scholastic Corporation.

Yes!

American women have been struggling for equal rights for many decades. Now they have the right to vote, get elected to public office, and hold top positions in business and the professions. In peacetime they are the equal of men—why not in wartime?

It would be easy to work out. We're not proposing that women handle bazookas or drive tanks. But there are hundreds of other military tasks. The army has only to total up the womanpower it needs, just as it figures up its manpower requirements. There's practically no limit to the valuable jobs women can do in uniform. The Army Nurse Corps, for instance, has been in operation for almost fifty years. Everyone recognizes the special talents that women have for nursing. But what about typing, stenography, bookkeeping, operating a switchboard? The armed forces ought to have women available to fill these jobs too.

But that's only the beginning. What about pharmacist's mates, cooks, bakers, parachute riggers, movie technicians, radio operators, drivers, code experts, flight control radio operators? These were assignments held by some women in World War II. They proved that they could do these jobs as well, *or better*, than men. Practically every one of those jobs could have been held by women. . . .

Note that we said that women can handle some jobs better than men. Yes, it's true, even in the army. For example, as radio communications workers, women's voices are clearer and normally do not become as garbled as men's voices. . . .

" For the particular tasks for which the woman is particularly qualified in war, she is far better than any man in the army," [states] . . . General of the Army Dwight D. Eisenhower.

Some people think it odd that we haven't drafted women before. Many single men are the sole support of their parents. This is far less true for single women. Many young men, training to be doctors, lawyers, or engineers, require years of education and practice before they can earn a living and support a family. Military service for them is a real, often permanent, sacrifice of their careers. But this is hardly as true for most

UNIVERSAL CONSCRIPTION

women (with due respect for the small proportion of women in the professions). A few years of military service might interrupt a woman's job, but it hardly is likely to do permanent harm to her career.

Everyone wants to do his part for his country. But it's also true that people become uncertain when they're not called to duty. They don't really know where they are needed. Right now, the army needs thousands of doctors. But many doctors aren't volunteering because they honestly don't know whether they are more valuable on the home front or in the armed services. Once the draft of doctors begins, medical men will recognize their obligation to the armed services.

The same is true of women. Many of them said to themselves in World War II, "I'd sign up tomorrow if I knew I was needed. But if the army really wanted women, they'd draft them." In other words, we have millions of women ready to don uniforms, if and when they're told to.

Today the United Nations is at war with the forces of Communist aggression. The Communists, in Russia and elsewhere, do not hesitate to put their women into the front line. Can we afford not to draft our women in the desperate fight we face in the months and years ahead?

Says one of our outstanding Congresswomen, Representative Frances P. Bolton of Ohio:

> By giving women an equal place in our armed forces, the last exclusively male profession, we shall be opening a new career field to them in time of peace and recognizing their obligation in time of war. When our house is burning down, let's revise the old saying that a woman's place is in the home. Let's realize that today a woman's place includes the saving of that home.

No!

... There are many reasons against drafting women. The most important reason is the part women play in family life. When we are at war, we do service to the enemy and disservice to ourselves if we unnecessarily disrupt our whole way of life. During war, we would not think of closing our schools or using our churches as warehouses. We know that, in wartime perhaps more than in peacetime, we must continue to educate youngsters for the future and to permit all people to worship as they choose.

In much the same way, we must not destroy or weaken the basic institution of the family. It is one thing to permit single women without family responsibilities to volunteer for the armed forces. It is quite another to draft women—the mothers, daughters, or sisters of men in the armed forces or in defense industries.

A soldier's main source of hope and encouragement is that he will return, after the bitter business of war, to the home he left behind him. Take Bill Jones, 23-year-old army draftee. As he goes to war, he leaves at home his parents, his unmarried sister, and the wife he married only months ago. He wants to think that his sister will remain at home to take care of his parents—not only financially, but also to keep them in good spirits and to cushion them against the shocks that war can bring. And Bill wants his wife safe at home, too. Perhaps she will work for the Red Cross or even in a war factory. But, Bill believes, she should be devoting her spare time to planning for the future Jones' home and preparing herself for family life.

What happens to Bill's dreams if his sister and wife are drafted? You answer that one for yourself! Of course, there are a few "Bill Joneses" who want their wives or sisters to join them in the service. For these women, the answer is simple. They may volunteer.

We know that the women who have *volunteered* for the armed services during and since World War II are highly capable and cooperative, ready to do exactly as they are told. But what happens if we *draft* women—including thousands who have no interest in joining the armed forces? Can we be at all sure that women draftees will measure up to the high standards set by women volunteers? There is no assurance of this in advance.

In drafting women, it would be just as difficult as in drafting men to decide who shall be called and who shall stay home. Among the things Uncle Sam considers in drafting a man are his family status (how many people are dependent upon him) and his occupation (is his defense job more important than service in the army). These vary from case to case. However, selective service headquarters can say, for instance, that the draft will not take those with more than two dependents or those who are in any one of seventy-five vital defense jobs.

Drafting women would present the same kinds of difficulties. First, of course, you exempt mothers of young children. But, then, how do you proceed? Do you draft one soldier's wife, but not another's? Do you take a single girl, about to be married and about to start a family, and leave at home another single girl who may have a defense job? You are dealing in matters which cannot be tied down to easily applied rules.

Much has been said about what other nations are doing. Let's take another look at this. Britain was fighting for her very life in World War II. Every woman from 18 to 50 had to register for vital war work. But women were not required to go into the armed forces. They were offered the choice of farm work, nursing, civil defense, *or* the armed forces.

America's present position is hardly as serious as that of Britain in World War II. How can we consider so serious a step as drafting women, when our British cousins, for good reasons, did not do so in their desperate emergency?

As for Russia's action in putting women into the front lines, it would be foolish to imitate the Communists. The Russians also send political opponents to Siberia. Does anybody suggest we ought to imitate this, too?

If an American girl thinks she can serve her country best in the armed forces, let her volunteer. But let's not delude ourselves into drafting her away from her time-honored place on the home front.

IF WOMEN ARE DRAFTED [6]

There's a great deal of talk in Washington today about how women may react to being drafted in wartime. But the women themselves, it seems to me are actually way ahead of the Washington officials in their thinking; with typical realism they're already wondering not *if* they will be drafted, but *what jobs* they will be drafted for.

How right they are! For if war does come women will almost certainly be drafted for military service, work in war industries and civil defense jobs—and on just about the same basis as men. . . .

[6] From an article by Major George Fielding Eliot, military analyst. *Woman's Home Companion.* 78:34-5+. February 1951. Reprinted by permission.

The plans now under way are reasonably clear. The British experience—full details are public property—is being followed in general. So it's possible to give you quite a good idea of what's in store . . . if those plans are ever translated into stern reality.

For men and women alike there will be four general categories of war service: (1) military service; (2) civilian employment in the government; (3) civilian employment in essential war industry; (4) civil defense.

It's likely that if you're a single woman or a childless widow or divorcée between the ages of 19 and 30, you will have to go into military service if you can meet the rather severe physical requirements. You will have a choice between the WAC (women's army corps), WAF (women in the air force), the navy's WAVES, the Coast Guard's SPARS and the women marines. . . .

The main function of women in uniform will be to release men for combat duty overseas. Any job a woman can possibly do will not be allowed to absorb a man capable of combat service. If we must fight Russia we'll hope to fight on the same strategic principle we used against Germany and Japan—use our command of the sea to keep the ground fighting on enemy soil. But any fighting on distant battlefields needs a sturdy base organization of services and administration at home—and also in overseas base areas. Women can be used for thousands of these jobs.

In 1945, when the last war ended, we had about 200,000 WACs, WAVES and women marines. If war comes again it's a good guess that there'll be something like 2.5 million women in the army alone and another million in the navy, marines, air force and Coast Guard. These figures, far more than any words, give you an idea of the tremendous responsibilities which women in uniform will have to bear in the winning of another victory.

Will women actually fight? Probably not in the front lines—as Russian women have. But British women served effectively in anti-aircraft units at home, which is certainly fighting, and American women may do the same. Furthermore a war with the Soviet Union would probably include guerrilla warfare behind our own lines—as our boys found out in Korea—in which every cook, clerk, truckdriver and hospital attendant has to drop his (or her) work at a split-second alarm and grab a carbine or man a machine gun to fight off sudden attack. Right now our women in uniform are being taught to use weapons. The marines do it openly; the other services do it under the guise of "participation in outdoor sports." . . .

Women serving overseas will have to be trained to defend themselves in an emergency. This necessity is underlined by the fact that women soldiers who fall into enemy hands can expect little consideration.

Much of the navy's shore establishment will be manned by WAVES, relieving men for sea duty. In the air force, women will handle maintenance, communications, weather reporting, supply and medical duties and many other jobs not directly involving flight. Will there be women pilots? Probably, for ferry duties and for transport and other noncombat aircraft. General Hoyt S. Vandenberg, Air Force Chief of Staff, strongly hinted at a recent congressional hearing that such use of women was planned.

Before turning to the civilian side of the picture we should mention nurses, medical specialists and women doctors. There is a critical shortage of nurses, likely to become desperate if war breaks out. No young woman draftee who is a graduate nurse has a chance of being assigned to anything else. If you're drafted and have had any nursing training at all, you will almost surely be sent to school to become a full-fledged nurse. It's quite likely that nursing will have a priority on all the younger draftees; any girl having certain educational and temperamental qualifications will be sent to nurses' training school whether she wants to go or not. There are advantages to being a nurse—for example, they're all commissioned officers.

The same applies to medical specialists (dietitians, physical and occupational therapists). They'll have commissions laid in their laps. As for women doctors and dentists, it's quite probable that they'll serve—as officers, of course—at sea or in overseas hospitals on much the same basis as men doctors.

Incidentally, you won't have to be a nurse or a doctor to get a commission. If you have had two years of college, you'll probably be able to apply for officer-candidate school as soon as you've completed basic training in any of the women's services. You'll go to the school right along with the men; at least in the air force that's happening already. "It keeps both men and women on their toes," an air force general told me.

While today women can't advance above the rank of lieutenant colonel or commander, except for the heads of the various women's services, this restriction is virtually certain to disappear in wartime. Female generals and admirals—strange as that may sound to you—are sure to come with the drafting of millions of women into uniform.

But if war comes women in uniform will be only a small fraction of the draft. Of the estimated 31 million women between the ages of 19 and 50 in the United States, only about one tenth—perhaps a little more—are likely to find their way into military service. What will be the war duties of the others?

Many, of course, will hold down technical, scientific, administrative and specialist jobs in the government or will work in essential war industries. Some will already be in such jobs when called up by the draft; most of these will be left where they are if their work is certified as essential. Others who are capable of doing such work will be drafted into it. Still others will be sent to training schools to fit them for such duties—to learn stenography, for example; already there is a critical shortage of stenographers in Washington.

But it's a fair guess that the vast majority of women drafted into full-time jobs will not go to an office. They'll be assigned to a factory, shipyard or aircraft assembly plant. Many will need training, which they'll get mostly on the job, though some will attend special classes.

Drafting women as well as men for wartime labor, compelling them by law to take and stick to jobs to which they are assigned is not, we'll all agree, a happy prospct. But Britain was forced to it in World War II. Parliament authorized the government "to direct any person of any age in the United Kingdom to perform any service within the United Kingdom which that person is capable of performing."

UNIVERSAL CONSCRIPTION

The British people swallowed this bitter pill because it was a question of organizing all their resources or going under. That will be the question with us too if there is war with the Soviet Union.

There will be, of course, exceptions to these general rules. No mother with young children to care for will be eligible for military service, nor will she be drafted into any job which will take her from her children. There is no use fighting to preserve a society if you start breaking the basic fiber of the very thing you're trying to protect. Nevertheless a mother may be assigned to a part-time office or factory job in the vicinity of her home, if suitable care can be arranged for her children while she is at work. Such care was offered in Britain by volunteers—women too old for the draft or physically unfit for working or fighting—and their work was of great value.

Probably most mothers will be drafted into the civil defense corps—but take it from the experience of British mothers, that can get rough. Each woman, for the most part, will work part time. Teams of two, three or four will be assigned to each post. Mothers may take turns caring for each other's children while one of their number mans their post.

If you're a mother here's a sample of the kind of job you may be assigned to: control center, communications, air raid warning service, aircraft observer, warden or assistant warden, decontamination, evacuation, sanitation and public health, truck driver, traffic policewoman, first aid, welfare, personnel administration.

Make no mistake, these are tough, exacting jobs. We played around with civil defense in the last war—remember the blackouts and sirens? But there was never any real danger of attack. Next time it will be bitterly different. Civil defense will not be play. Again, ask the British.

Whether it's building a cookstove from rubble so that there may be hot coffee for the homeless or shepherding dazed and devastated people; whether it's driving an ambulance through debris-strewn streets or the heart-rending task of enforcing priority rules in evacuating a city, the American woman who wears the civil-defense brassard on her arm will have no easy time of it. But like her British sister she'll stick it out.

When will all this happen? I don't know. But if a full-scale conflict comes, that's when women will be drafted. Congress is unlikely to pass any general draft law, especially a draft of women or a labor draft, until it has to.

There *may* be a general registration before that, though—a sort of survey of America's human resources. Those who argue for such a registration think we should take inventory right away. Those who oppose it feel that registration not immediately followed by a call to duty might produce a morale slump—people would get keyed up over registering and then when they weren't called immediately there'd be a reaction.

If women are drafted probably they'll be called in age groups, the younger women first. It's likely that the earliest draftees will have a choice between military service and civilian war jobs, or one of the permanent full-time posts in civil defense. Later on they may have less choice; the British found their war-industry needs became so great that they finally had to order all new draftees straight into overalls.

There'll be opposition to drafting women, of course. Much of it will come from men, to judge from all that has been said and written on the subject so far. One man who testified before a congressional committee on the subject of making the WAC permanent said bluntly: 'Women are bad for the army, the army is bad for women and the combination is bad for society." A letter writer to the New York *Times* wondered what we'd have to defend if we weren't defending our women. "Let our women be saved though the nation perish," he insisted with flourishing but hardly logical gallantry. . . .

There's some opposition among women too. Many girls recall a husband, brother or boy friend who frowned on WACs and WAVES and said, "Don't ever let me catch *you* in any uniform." These girls think they'll lose some of their feminine appeal as soldiers—or in overalls. There's no doubt that the male prejudice they fear does exist, but in the services themselves it's pleasant to know that the regular women officers and enlisted personnel who are now a permanent part of the army, navy and

UNIVERSAL CONSCRIPTION

air force have done a lot to eradicate the feeling. The same pleasant news is true of women workers in many a manufacturing plant. . . .

The majority of women with whom I've talked don't waste time deploring unpleasant facts. Surprisingly few try to hide behind such wishful thinking as, "A draft won't be needed; there'll be lots of volunteers." I'm convinced that women have been talking this thing over among themselves a lot more realistically . . . than most of us men suspect. There's a widespread understanding among them of such facts as:

1. We have almost no labor reserve except our thirty-odd million women.

2. War will require immense expansion of industrial production at the moment when millions of men are being called up for military service.

3. Without women civil defense could not be carried on at all and without civil defense we could not hope to survive serious enemy air attack.

4. Owing to the low birth rate of the depression years and the high percentage of rejections among male draftees today we can never have enough fighting men unless we use women for service and maintenance jobs in the armed forces.

5. We shall need *more* fighting men *more* quickly than in the last war because of the comparative weakness of our allies today.

6. Finally, the draft is the only efficient and fair way of making the best use of our human resources, male and female.

BIBLIOGRAPHY

An asterisk (*) preceding a reference indicates that the article or a part of it has been reprinted in this book.

BIBLIOGRAPHIES

Princeton University. Manpower and personnel problems in industrial mobilization. (Selected References. no37) 8p. The University. Industrial Relations Section. Princeton, N.J. '50.

Princeton University. Manpower problem in the present emergency. (Selected References. no35) 4p. The University. Industrial Relations Section. Princeton, N.J. '50.

United States. Library of Congress. Division of Bibliography. Universal military training (Bibliography no1583). mimeo. Library of Congress. Washington 25, D.C. '45.

University of Illinois. High school youth and military service. (Labor-Management Relations. v3, no6) 7p. mimeo. The University. Institute of Labor and Industrial Relations. 704 S. 6th St. Champaign, Ill. '51.

University of Illinois. Labor in the crisis. (Labor-Management Relations. v3, no4) 6p. mimeo. The University. Institute of Labor and Industrial Relations. 704 S. 6th St. Champaign, Ill. '50.

BOOKS AND PAMPHLETS

Aly, Bower, ed. War service: the twenty-fifth annual debate handbook. 2v. Lucas Bros. Columbia, Mo. '51.

American Friends Service Committee. Experience of the American Friends service committee in civilian public service. 51p. The Committee. Philadelphia. '45.

Armstrong, P. G. and others. Should college students be drafted? (Reviewing Stand. v16, no12) 12p. Northwestern University Radio Dept. Evanston, Ill. '51.

Atherton, W. H. and Carey, J. B. Should a national service act be adopted? (Town Meeting. v9, no37) 23p. Town Hall, Inc. 123 W. 43d St. New York 18. '44.

Bacon, F. L. and others. Analysis of the report of the President's advisory commission on universal training. 28p. National Council Against Conscription. 1013 18th St. Washington 6, D.C. '47.

*Bishop, P. W. Proposed national labor draft. 4p. Oberlin College Publicity Bureau. Oberlin, Ohio. '44.

UNIVERSAL CONSCRIPTION

Bosley, H. A. and others. Should 18-year-olds be soldiers? 5p. National Council Against Conscription. 1013 18th St. Washington 6, D.C. '51.

*British Information Services. Compulsory military service in Britain (ID 1041). 6p. mimeo. British Information Services. 30 Rockefeller Plaza. New York 20. '51.

British Information Services. Control of manpower in Britain. 18p. British Information Services. 30 Rockefeller Plaza. New York 20. '45.

*(British) Ministry of Labor and National Service. Report for the years 1939-46. 394p. H. M. Stationery Office. London. '47.

Chamber of Commerce of the United States. Committee on Economic Policy. Economic policies for national defense. 36p. The Chamber. Washington 6, D.C. '51.

Chartener, W. H. Manpower controls. (v2 '50, no7) 20p. Editorial Research Reports. 1205 19th St. Washington 6, D.C. '50.

Clay, L. D. and others. Manpower crisis. (University of Chicago Round Table. no235) 28p. University of Chicago Round Table. Chicago 37. '45.

Cocke, Erle, Jr. and Pickett, C. E. Universal military training. (American Forum of the Air. v13, no51) 11p. Ransdell, Inc. 810 Rhode Island Ave. Washington 18, D.C. '50.

Corson, J. J. Manpower for victory. 299p. Farrar and Rinehart. New York. '43.

*Devan, S. A. Universal military training and the problem of military manpower. (Public Affairs Bulletin. no90) 78p. Library of Congress. Legislative Reference Service. Washington, D.C. '51.

Einstein, Albert and others. Militarization of America. 32p. National Council Against Conscription. 1013 18th St. Washington 6, D.C. '48.

Einstein, Albert and others. New evidence of the militarization of America. 64p. National Council Against Conscription. 1013 18th St. Washington 6, D.C. '49.

Eliot, G. F. and others. Is universal military training necessary for our security? (Town meeting. v13, no12) 24p. Town Hall, Inc. 123 W. 43d St. New York 18. '47.

*Elliott, W. Y. Mobilization planning and the national security (1950-60). (Senate Document no204. 81st Congress, 2d session) 245p. Supt. of Docs. Washington 25, D.C. '50.

*Fitzpatrick, E. A. Universal military training. 374p. McGraw-Hill Book Co. New York. '45.

Gingerich, Melvin. Service for peace. 508p. Mennonite Central Committee. Akron, Pa. '49.

Ginzberg, Eli. Manpower policy for a readiness economy. Address delivered before Columbia College forum on democracy, February 25, 1951. Mimeographed text available from Columbia University. New York. '51.

Goodwin, R. C. Address delivered before Virginia Defense Mobilization Conference, Richmond, Va., February 2, 1951. Mimeographed text available from Department of Labor. Washington 25, D.C. '51.

Hart, I. W. Outline of historical background of selective service. 30p. Selective Service System. Washington 25, D.C. '48.

*Hershey, L. B. Statement before Preparedness Subcommittee, Committee on Armed Services, U. S. Senate, January 18, 1951. Mimeographed text available from Selective Service System. Washington 25, D.C. '51.

Hershey, L. B. and Short, Dewey. Draft act. (American Forum of the air. v13, no9) 12p. Ransdell, Inc. 810 Rhode Island Ave. Washington 18, D.C. '51.

Hershey, L. B. and others. Do we need universal military training? (American Forum of the Air. v9, no24) 11p. Ransdell, Inc. 810 Rhode Island Ave. Washington 18, D.C. '47.

Hershey, L. B. and others. Who should be drafted? (Reviewing Stand. v15, no15) 11p. Northwestern University Radio Dept. Evanston, Ill. '50.

Huddle, F. P. Universal service. (v 1 '44, no15) 19p. Editorial Research Reports. 1205 19th St. Washington 6, D.C. '44.

Johnsen, J. E. Compulsory military training. (Reference Shelf. v14, no6) 266p. H. W. Wilson Co. New York. '41.
Bibliography.

Johnson, E. D. and others. Should we establish a system of universal military training? (American Forum of the Air. v9, no10) 15p. Ransdell, Inc. 810 Rhode Island Ave. Washington 18, D.C. '47.

King, S. B. Selective service in North Carolina in World War II. 451p. University of North Carolina Press. Chapel Hill. '49.

McNickle, R. K. Education in an extended emergency. (v 1 '51, no9) 17p. Editorial Research Reports. 1205 19th St. Washington 6, D.C. '51.

McNickle, R. K. Medical manpower. (v 1 '51, no6) 16p. Editorial Research Reports. 1205 19th St. Washington 6, D.C. '51.

McNickle, R. K. Training for war service. (v2 '50, no17) 20p. Editorial Research Reports. 1205 19th St. Washington 6, D.C. '50.

McNickle, R. K. Womanpower in mobilization. (v 1 '51, no3) 17p. Editorial Research Reports. 1205 19th St. Washington 6, D.C. '51.

Maverick, Maury and others. Should Congress pass a work or fight bill? (Town Meeting. v10, no40) 24p. Town Hall, Inc. 123 W. 43d St. New York 18. '45.

May, A. J. and others. Do we need "work or fight" legislation? (American Forum of the Air. v7, no5) 15p. Ransdell, Inc. 810 Rhode Island Ave. Washington 18, D.C. '45.

*National Council Against Conscription. Cost of universal military training. 5p. The Council. 1013 18th St. Washington 6, D.C. '51.

National Council Against Conscription. We dare not risk another army mistake. 16p. The Council. 1013 18th St. Washington 6, D.C. '48.

National Security Resources Board. Scientific Manpower Advisory Committee. Plans for the development and use of scientific manpower. 16p. The Board. Washington 25, D.C. '51.

Pacifist Research Bureau. Conscientious objectors in World War II. (Quarterly research survey. no 1) 19p. The Bureau. 316 E. Court St. Ithaca, N.Y. '49.

Spencer, W. H. and others. Do we need compulsory manpower legislation? (Reviewing Stand. v4, no13) 11p. Northwestern University Radio Dept. Evanston, Ill. '45.

Summers, R. E. and Summers, H. B. Universal military service. (Reference Shelf. v15, no2) 280p. H. W. Wilson Co. '41.
  Bibliography.

Taylor, R. L. Farm manpower. (v 1 '51, no13) 16p. Editorial Research Reports. 1205 19th St. Washington 6, D.C. '51.

*Truman, Harry S. National manpower mobilization policy, January 17, 1951. 6p. Mimeographed text available from the White House. Washington 25, D.C. '51.

Trytten, M. H. and others. Report of the six scientific advisory committees on deferment of students. 30p. mimeo. Selective Service System. Washington 25, D.C. '50.

*United States. Congress. Special Senate Committee Investigating the National Defense Program. Third annual report (no10, part 16) 582p. Supt. of Docs. Washington, D.C. '44.

United States. Congress. Universal military training. **Hearings before the Committee on Armed Services, House of Representatives.** 969p. 82d Congress, 1st session. Supt. of Docs. Washington 25, D.C. '51.

*United States. Congress. Universal military training and service act. (House of Representatives report no535) 27p. 82d Congress, 1st session. Washington 25, D.C. '51.

United States. Congress. Universal military training and service act of 1951. Hearings before the Preparedness Subcommittee of the Senate Committee on Armed Services. 1243p. 82d Congress, 1st session. Supt. of Docs. Washington 25, D.C. '51.

*United States. Department of Labor. Nation-wide labor-management manpower set-up activated. Press release of the Department, dated May 1, 1951. The Department. Washington 25, D.C. '51.

United States. Department of Labor. Bureau of Labor Statistics. Fact book on manpower. 77p. Supt. of Docs. Washington 25, D.C. '51.

United States. Department of Labor. Bureau of Labor Statistics. Manpower report no7. 15p. mimeo. The Bureau. Washington 25, D.C. '51.

*United States. Department of Labor. Women's Bureau. The role of women in wartime Britain, 1939-45; prepared by Margaret M. Fitzpatrick. 16p. The Bureau. Washington 25, D.C. '50.

United States. Office of War Information. Report by War Manpower Commission's management-labor policy committee, November 6, 1943 (PM-4460). 8p. mimeo. Supt. of Docs. Washington 25, D.C. '43.

*United States. President's Advisory Commission on Universal Training. A program for national security. 447p. Supt. of Docs. Washington 25, D.C. '47.

*Wertz, L. R. Manpower mobilization. Address delivered before Steel Founders Society of America, Chicago, March 20, 1951. Mimeographed text available from the Department of Labor. Washington 25, D.C. '51.

*Wilson, C. E. Building America's might (first quarterly report of Office of Defense Mobilization). 43p. Supt. of Docs. Washington 25, D.C. '51.

Yoder, Dale. Manpower economics and labor problems. 661p. McGraw-Hill Book Co. New York. '50.

Periodicals

American Federationist. 58:3-5. F. '51. AFL Council backs limited UMT.

American Magazine. 134:18-19+. D. '42. You and your family will be mobilized. Harry Hopkins.
    Same condensed. Reader's Digest. 42:7-10. F. '43.

American Magazine. 147:47+. Je. '49. Women should be drafted. F. P. Bolton.

American Psychologist. 5:641-2. N. '50. Manpower utilization under the Selective service act. E. L. Kelly.

American School Board Journal. 122:39+. My. '51. Military deferment of college students. E. A. Fitzpatrick.

American Sociological Review. 11:85-9. F. '46. Wartime controls in a democratic society. E. C. McVoy.

*American Sociological Review. 15:534-45. Ag. '50. Wartime manpower controls in Japan. E. C. McVoy.

Annals of the American Academy of Political and Social Sciences. 241:1-168. S. '45. Universal military training and national security.

UNIVERSAL CONSCRIPTION 173

Army Information Digest. 2:3-7. Je. '47. Men, money and UMT. R. S. McLain.
Army Information Digest. 2:9-44. Je. '47. A report on UMT.
Business Week. p 19-20. S. 9, '50. Manpower: no big reserve, but enough.
Business Week. p25. O. 14, '50. Skills: for army or industry?
Business Week. p31-2+. N. 11, '50. What to do about manpower.
Business Week. p 19-20. Ja. 20, '51. Universal training at age 18.
Business Week. p 100+. Ja. 20, '51. Colleges in trouble.
Business Week. p 128+. F. 10, '51. Who'll mobilize manpower?
Business Week. p23. F. 17, '51. Manpower policy: draft 'em.
Business Week. p 113-20. F. 17, '51. How to live with controls.
Christian Century. 67:197. F. 15, '50. It's conscription they want.
Christian Century. 67:388. Mr. 29, '50. Young c. o.'s threatened by new draft law.
Christian Century. 67:1092. S. 20, '50. Enlarged army raises issue of c. o.'s.
Christian Century. 67:1315. N. 8, '50. New developments in c. o. cases.
Christian Century. 68:101. Ja. 24, '51. Educators deserve support on draft.
Christian Science Monitor. p 16. F. 14, '51. Confusion over mobilization of women. Josephine Ripley.
Commercial and Financial Chronicle. 172:1991+. N. 23, '50. Planning to meet manpower needs. R. C. Goodwin.
Commercial and Financial Chronicle. 173:254-5+. Ja. 18, '51. Manpower situation. E. L. Keenan.
Commonweal. 41:363-4. Ja. 26, '45. National service act debate.
Commonweal. 52:453-4. Ag. 18, '50. What is essential?
Congressional Digest. 23:101-27. Ap. '44. Should the U. S. adopt civilian conscription for war?
Congressional Digest. 24:3-32. Ja. '45. Should the United States adopt compulsory peacetime military training?
Congressional Digest. 26:225-56. O. '45. An historic decision for Congress: UMT for U. S. A.?
*Congressional Record. 90:A1326-7. Mr. 15, '44. Opposition to national service act. C. W. Vursell.
*Current History. 6:243-9. Mr. '44. Message to Congress. F. D. Roosevelt.
   Same. Vital Speeches of the Day. 10:194-7. Ja. 15, '44.
Factory Management and Maintenance. p70-3. S. '50. Coming crisis in manpower. M. J. Murphy.
Fortune. 42:45-6. N. '50. Manpower arithmetic.
Fortune. 43:78-9+. Mr. '51. Manpower controls next?
Fortune. 43:79+. Mr. '51. Resources and requirements for a $65-billion posture.

Harper's Bazaar. 85:146-7+. Ap. '51. The case for UMT. W. C. Menninger.

Harper's Magazine. 190:289-300. Mr. '45. Conscription for peacetime? H. W. Baldwin.

Harper's Magazine. 202:30-3. Mr. '51. Exempt the bright boys? G. W. Johnson.

Higher Education. 7:167. Mr. 15, '51. Military service and deferment for students in England.

Independent Woman. 23:91-2. Mr. '44. National service act: pro and con.

Independent Woman. 30:101-2. Ap. '51. Womanpower and the draft. G. F. McQuatters.

Independent Woman. 30:113. Ap. '51. Women should be drafted. S. T. Hughes.

Journal of the American Association of University Women. 44:141-4. Spring. '51. Drafting women for the armed forces. M. M. Horton.

Labor and Nation. p26-7. Summer '50. Labor and the military. Kermit Eby.

Labor Market and Employment Security. Ag. 25, '50. Manpower potential for national security.

Ladies' Home Journal. 68:53. F. '51. Why not draft women? M. M. Horton.

Law and Contemporary Problems. 9:458-9. Summer '42. Some legal aspects of wartime labor mobilization. Bernice Lotwin and R. G. Conley.

Law and Contemporary Problems. 9:523-5. Summer '42. Wartime methods of dealing with labor in Great Britain and the Dominions. M. H. Schoenfeld and A. L. Whitney.

Law and Contemporary Problems. 9:544-66. Summer '42. Labor mobilization in Nazi Germany. Franz Neumann.

*Look. 14:33-5. D. 19, '50. A stern program for survival. J. B. Conant.

*Look. 15:54-5. Ja. 2, '51. Total conscription will hurt America. C. W. Cole.

Look. 15:sub 1-2. Mr. 13, '51. College draft deferment plan. R. C. Myers.

Monthly Labor Review. 59:264-78. Ag. '44. Sources of wartime labor supply in the United States. Leonard Eskin.

Monthly Labor Review. 71:359. S. '50. Selective service extension provisions.

Monthly Labor Review. 71:564-7. N. '50. Labor-supply aspects of mobilization. M. J. Tobin.

Monthly Labor Review. 71:575. N. '50. Office of defense manpower in Department of labor.

Monthly Labor Review. 72:257-62, 385-90. Mr.-Ap. '51. Elements of Soviet labor law. Vladimir Gsovski.

Nation. 158:190-1. Ja. 22, '44. F. D. R. and national service. I. F. Stone.
Nation. 158:123-4. Ja. 29, '44. Facts for Mr. Stimson. I. F. Stone.
Nation. 171:685. D. 30, '50. Shape of things: college students and the draft.
Nation. 172:124-6. F. 10, '51. Manpower balance sheet. Keith Hutchison.
Nation. 172:154-6. F. 17, '51. Right people in the right place. Keith Hutchison.
National Education Association Journal. 49:15-16. Ja. '51. Mobilization and education. J. K. Little.
Nation's Business. 38:31-2+. O. '50. When war takes your employes. J. W. Whittlesey.
*Nation's Business. 39:31-3+. Ja. '51. How fair is the draft? Stanley Frank.
Nation's Business. 39:32-4+. Ap. '51. Should we draft our women? Milton Lehman and Mildred Lehman.
New Republic. 124:7-8. Ja. 29, '51. Uniforms for all.
*New York Post. p26. Ap. 3, '51. The army's big UMT offensive.
New York Post. p28. My. 15, '51. Nine million married women in jobs. S. F. Porter.
New York Times. p 1. Mr. 12, '51. Graham named to manpower job.
New York Times. p7. Ap. 4, '51. Deferment idea faulty. H. W. Baldwin.
New York Times. p E9. Ap. 8, '51. Draft deferment policy. Benjamin Fine.
New York Times. p4. Ap. 9, '51. Services waste skills. H. W. Baldwin.
New York Times. p71. Ap. 29, '51. Fading manpower worries farmers. W. M. Blair.
New York Times. p 12. Je. 4, '51. UMT plan questioned. H. W. Baldwin.
New York Times. p 1+. Je. 8, '51. Draft compromise passed by Congress. H. B. Hinton.
New York Times. p 16. Je. 13, '51. 395,000 will lose deferment under new draft law.
*New York Times Magazine. p 17+. O. 1, '50. Our great unused resource, womanpower. D. C. Stratton.
New York Times Magazine. p 11+. Mr. 4, '51. The 18-year-old: an indistinct portrait. D. L. Farnsworth.
*New York Times Magazine. p 12+. My. 13, '51. Making the most of manpower. J. J. Corson.
New York Times Magazine. p 15+. My. 27, '51. Service stripes and college grades. W. C. Fels.
Newsweek. 36:20. D. 4, '50. Universal service is needed. E. K. Lindley.

Newsweek. 37:22. Ja. 29, '51. Wanted: many hands; manpower mobilization policy.
Occupations. 29:431-3. Mr. '51. Manpower, a 1951 management problem. F. H. Kirkpatrick.
*Parents' Magazine. p26-7+. Ja. '51. Should we have universal military training? Fletcher Pratt and A. F. Myers.
Reporter. p 12-14. Ag. 29, '50. U. S. manpower. H. H. Landsberg.
Russian Review. 8:117-26. Ap. '49. Universal military service in Russia and Western Europe. A. M. Nikolaieff.
*Saturday Evening Post. 223:29+. S. 16, '50. What will we be short of this time? P. F. Drucker.
Saturday Evening Post. 223:28-9+. Ja. 20, '51. Who will be drafted this time? Sam Stavisky.
School and Society. 73:28. Ja. 13, '51. AASA committee on military service and training.
School and Society. 73:65-8. F. 3, '51. National defense and the complete development of our human resources; college military camps for universal training. W. W. Kemmerer.
School Review. 58:384-6. O. '50. Youths facing military service: schooling as usual? R. C. Woellner.
School Review. 59:8-9. Ja. '51. Selective service and higher education. Norman Burns.
Science. 112:349-52. S. 29, '50. Scientists and mobilization. Wadsworth Likely.
Science. 112:479-83. O. 20, '50. Students, scientists, and selective service: joint report of the scientific advisory committees.
Science. 113:sup3. Ja. 19, '51. Scientific manpower. Wadsworth Likely.
Science. 113:sup3. Mr. 16, '51. Use of manpower: AAAS resolution. H. A. Meyerhoff.
Science News Letter. 58:114. Ag. 19, '50. Danger in mobilization.
Science News Letter. 58:216. S. 30, '50. MIT head urges total draft if total war.
Science News Letter. 58:421-2+. D. 30, '50. Plan for brainpower; symposium.
Senior Scholastic. 44:3-4. F. 7, '44. Shall we draft everybody?
Senior Scholastic. 45:5-6. Ja. 22, '45. Congress grapples with manpower problem.
Senior Scholastic. 57:11-13. S. 27, '50. Manpower, the muscles of defense. H. L. Marx, Jr.
*Senior Scholastic. 57:18-19. S. 27, '50. Should Uncle Sam draft women? H. L. Marx, Jr.
Senior Scholastic. 57:10-12. Ja. 10, '51. How will you fit in? H. L. Marx, Jr.
*Senior Scholastic. 58:12-13. Ap. 25, '51. Should superior college students be deferred? H. L. Marx, Jr.

UNIVERSAL CONSCRIPTION

*State Government. 23:267-70+. D. '50. Selective service: history and functions. P. G. Armstrong.
Survey. 87:106-9. Mr. '51. Service in times of crisis. A. A. Berle and others.
Survey. 87:165-6. Ap. '51. What is your draft status? R. F. Reddin.
United States News & World Report. 29:38, 20-1. Ag. 11-18, '50. Who can get deferments?
United States News & World Report. 29:24-5. Ag. 25, '50. When universal training comes.
United States News & World Report. 29:40-1. S. 1, '50. Pinch in skilled-labor supply.
United States News & World Report. 29.34-8. S. 29, '50. Predicting draft trends. L. B. Hershey.
United States News & World Report. 29:13-14. N. 24, '50. Who works, who fights? task of Mrs. Rosenberg.
United States News & World Report. 30:24-5. Ja. 5, '51. Draft, who goes in '51?
United States News & World Report. 30:18-19. Ja. 12, '51. Tug of war for 18-year-olds.
United States News & World Report. 30:22-3. Ja. 19, '51. Universal service: what it means.
United States News & World Report. 30:32-6. F. 2, '51. Effects of new draft. A. M. Rosenberg.
United States News & World Report. 30:28-9. F. 9, '51. Congress asks: does army waste men?
United States News & World Report. 30:11-13. Ap. 13, '51. The new draft: study or fight.
Vital Speeches of the Day. 9:2-5. O. 15, '42. Manpower and the second front. F. D. Roosevelt.
Vital Speeches of the Day. 9:505-8. Je. 1, '43. Progress in manpower utilization. P. V. McNutt.
*Vital Speeches of the Day. 9:508-10. Je. 1, '43. Mobilization of manpower. J. W. Wadsworth, Jr.
*Vital Speeches of the Day. 10:258-61. F. 15, '44. Same liability for all. H. L. Stimson.
*Vital Speeches of the Day. 10:324-6. Mr. 15, '44. Austin-Wadsworth bill. William Green.
*Vital Speeches of the Day. 11:194-201. Ja. 15, '45. Message to Congress. F. D. Roosevelt.
  Same abridged. Current History. 8:253-4. Mr. '45.
Vital Speeches of the Day. 11:295-7. Mr. 1, '45. Adopt national service legislation now. H. L. Stimson.
Vital Speeches of the Day. 11:297-9. Mr. 1, '45. Job ahead for industry. Ira Mosher.

Vital Speeches of the Day. 16:367-8. Ap. 1, '50. Insurance for peace; extension of selective service. L. B. Hershey.
Vital Speeches of the Day. 17:305-8. Mr. 1, '51. Present danger. J. B. Conant.
*Woman's Home Companion. 78:34-5+. F. '51. If women are drafted. G. F. Eliot.

DEBATING

Competitive Debate... ...rategy. By G. M. ... 151p. rev. ed. 1946. $1.25.

Discussion Methods: Explained and Illustrated. By J. V. Garland. 376p. 3d ed. rev. 1951. $3.

Extempore Speaking: A Handbook for the Student, the Coach, and the Judge. By D. L. Holley. 115p. 1947. $1.50.

High School Forensics: An Integrated Program. By A. E. Melzer. 153p. 1940. 90c.

How to Debate. By H. B. Summers, F. L. Whan, and T. A. Rousse. rev. ed. 349p. 1950. $2.75.

Representative American Speeches. By A. C. Baird, comp. Published annually in The Reference Shelf. Prices vary.

Each volume contains representative speeches by eminent men and women on public occasions during the year. Each speech is prefaced by a short sketch of the speaker and the occasion.

Selected Readings in Rhetoric and Public Speaking. By Lester Thonssen, comp. 324p. 1942. $3.

UB
353
M34

This book may be kept

7 Days

only

It Cannot Be Renewed
Because of special demand